SNIFFER

THE LIFE AND TIMES OF ALLAN CLARKE

To my daughter, Sarah, and son, James, for making me a proud man.

SNIFFER
THE LIFE AND TIMES OF ALLAN CLARKE

David Saffer

TEMPUS

First published 2001

PUBLISHED IN THE UNITED KINGDOM BY:

Tempus Publishing Ltd
The Mill, Brimscombe Port
Stroud, Gloucestershire GL5 2QG

PUBLISHED IN THE UNITED STATES OF AMERICA BY:

Tempus Publishing Inc.
2A Cumberland Street
Charleston, SC 29401

Tempus books are available in France and Germany
from the following addresses:

Tempus Publishing Group	Tempus Publishing Group
21 Avenue de la République	Gustav-Adolf-Straße 3
37300 Joué-lès-Tours	99084 Erfurt
FRANCE	GERMANY

British Library Cataloguing in Publication Data.
A catalogue record for this book is available from the British Library.

ISBN 0 7524 2168 9

Typesetting and origination by Tempus Publishing.
PRINTED AND BOUND IN GREAT BRITAIN.

CONTENTS

PREFACE

When I look back at my playing career, I feel I have been very fortunate. I could not have had a better apprenticeship than at Walsall, before Fulham gave me the opportunity to make a name for myself in the First Division. Two British transfer records then saw me join Leicester City, where I spent a season, before Don Revie brought me to Leeds United in 1969.

Working under the gaffer for five seasons, I had the most prolific period of my career and won all my major honours there. Naturally, one of my favourite memories was the FA Cup final win over Arsenal, but for me the greatest thrill was going in each day for training and playing week in week out with the likes of Billy Bremner and Mick Jones. On the international front I loved the challenge of competing against the great players of world football, and playing for Sir Alf Ramsey.

My time as a Football League manager at Barnsley (twice), Leeds and Scunthorpe certainly had its highs and lows, but I'm proud of what I achieved, especially seeing many young players go on to serve their clubs with distinction.

When David approached me about writing this biography, I was delighted to give my permission, because I knew it would be written in a style I would like. All the major stories of my football career are included and, as I requested, the book is statistically accurate and packed with illustrations. This was very important to me because it allows anyone to dip into different sections of the book depending on their favourite memory.

Finally, I'd like to thank Bobby Robson for his kind words in the foreword to this book. Bobby's had a tremendous career in football, and gave me a lot of advice when we played together at Fulham.

Putting this book together has brought back so many great memories for me; I hope it does for you too.

Allan Clarke
September 2001

INTRODUCTION

Allan Clarke was one of English football's great strikers of his generation, renowned at home and abroad as one of the most clinical finishers around. The second (and most famous) of five footballing brothers, his ruthless efficiency when one-on-one with any goalkeeper was extraordinary.

After making his debut at sixteen for Walsall, he honed his skills at Fulham, before British record transfers took him firstly to Leicester City, where he won the Man of the Match award in the 1969 FA Cup final, then to Leeds United as the hit man of Don Revie's great side – where he played alongside the likes of Billy Bremner, Jack Charlton, Norman Hunter, Peter Lorimer and Mick Jones.

Under Revie, 'Sniffer' Clarke had his finest years as a player, winning Championship, FA Cup and European honours. An all-time great at Leeds United, his winning strike in the 1972 Centenary FA Cup final, where again he won the Man of the Match award, is the single goal most cherished by Leeds supporters.

An England international, he scored on his debut in the 1970 World Cup before suffering the heartache of a World Cup exit to Poland in 1973. Of his 19 appearances for his country, arguably the most memorable was when he scored twice in a 5-0 win over Scotland at Hampden Park. As a manager, Allan led teams in all four divisions of the Football League – experiencing promotion, relegation, and numerous giant-killing acts in cup competitions.

In this profusely illustrated biography, Allan recalls the great matches he took part in and many of the characters and personalities that shaped his career. Thousands of boys fantasise about becoming a footballer, scoring the winning goal in an FA Cup final and playing for their country. Allan Clarke was one the few who achieved it.

Enjoy the memories.

David Saffer
September 2001

FOREWORD
BY BOBBY ROBSON

Towards the end of my playing days at Fulham, I played with Allan Clarke. It was obvious to me that he would make it as a top class striker. He was so sure of himself and oozed confidence. I remember in one game we had a vital penalty; I was the regular penalty taker and placed the ball on the spot. Suddenly there was a tap on my shoulder; it was Allan. He said, 'Take your time son' – I couldn't believe it. I was thirty-four and this nineteen-year-old, who'd just joined, tells me to take my time … he made me feel even more nervous! He had some nerve, but what a talent at that age.

Allan knew exactly where he was going in the game. He was confident and had tremendous self-belief in his own ability. If he had a poor match, it never worried him in the next one; he just played his best at all times.

Allan was a great taker of chances; he could literally smell a half-chance – so much so that he was nicknamed '*Sniffer*' Clarke. Although he had an instinctive awareness of an opportunity in the penalty box, he wasn't just a goal poacher, he was a goal scorer too and there is a difference. Not only could he finish off a move, he could do it on his own. Allan also had a *meanness* about him, which all great strikers have. Even if a colleague was better placed, if he fancied his chances he'd have a go … and rarely missed. Allan's forte was when he was one-on-one with a goalkeeper: you knew he'd score, he was so assured in that type of situation – so confident, so clinical.

Allan played in Don Revie's marvellous Leeds United side of the early 1970s and really blossomed into a world-class striker. His transfer from Leicester City to Leeds was a great move for him. Undoubtedly he was one of England's best forwards of his era and a brilliant taker of chances. If Allan Clarke was playing today, in my opinion he would be right up there with all the great strikers around in the game at the moment.

Having known Allan for many years, I know you will enjoy reminiscing about one of English football's great strikers.

Bobby Robson

ACKNOWLEDGEMENTS

I would like to thank Yorkshire Post Newspapers Ltd for supplying the majority of images for this book. I would also like to thank the following people and organisations for their help with this publication: Bobby Robson, Howard Dapin, Arthur Bower, John Staff, Jon Sanders and Lisa Collett. Thanks also to Mike Fisher at Yorkshire Post Newspapers and James Howarth and Rosie Knowles at Tempus Publishing. Every effort has been made to acknowledge the original source of copyright for all pictures. If anyone has any queries, please contact Tempus Publishing.

1
BORN FOR FOOTBALL
1946-1962

Allan Clarke was born on 31 July 1946. The third eldest of seven children, Allan grew up at 21 Johnson Road, Short Heath, Willenhall with his brothers and sisters: Venetia, Frank, Margaret, Derek, Kelvin and Wayne.

I enjoyed every minute of my childhood. Dad was a long-distance lorry driver who played centre forward at amateur level for Bangor City. Often he would be away from Monday to Friday, so Mum would be both parents to us. Although money was tight, none of us wanted for anything. Christmas time was always fantastic because I knew I'd get a new strip. I'd go straight outside and play football for hours.

As far back as I can remember, all I ever did was kick a ball about – whether in the back yard, local football pitch or at school. At New Invention Infant Junior School I was always getting told off for daydreaming in class, but when it came to football I was fine and spent every spare moment playing. If there was no ball we'd roll up old newspapers or use a tennis ball. I failed my eleven plus, so went to Short Heath Secondary Modern School. My school reports always had the same theme, 'If Allan had as much interest in his work as he has in football he would be top of the class.'

On the field I was making progress. I was playing and scoring regularly for Short Heath, including seven in a 12-1 win against Beacon School. In addition, I was also playing for Southeast Staffordshire District and Birmingham County Boys. Whichever team I represented, Mum always made sure my strip was clean for every match, and when my parents watched me they would never interfere like many parents; they just let me play and enjoy it. As long as I did my best that was great. I was very lucky. I had tremendous encouragement from all my family, including my brother-in-law, Les Cann, who offered me five shillings for every goal I scored against our local rivals, Dudley Boys. We won 8-0 and I scored four – Les never challenged me again after handing over my £1!

Throughout my school days I was known as 'Tiny' Clarke because of my height; I was still only four foot five when I left school. In many ways, my lack of height helped me because I was always in the thick of the action – scrapping for every ball – and it certainly developed my dribbling ability to get out of danger.

Over the years I won quite a few cups and one season Southeast Staffordshire got to the English Schools Trophy quarter-finals before losing to Worksop. It was a big game and all our parents came with on the coach journey to support us. We had a three-course meal before the game, which looking back is the last thing we needed

Allan aged two, with Frank and Venetia.

New Invention school team, 1955.

Allan with his Intermediate Shield gained with Southeast Staffordshire, 1957.

11

before a match!

Without question, I was from a family who loved sport and my parents were more than happy for all of us to pursue our interests. My elder sister, Venetia, didn't excel at a particular sport but loved following Walsall, whereas my younger sister, Margaret, was Southeast Staffordshire champion for sprint and long jump and won representative honours at netball.

When it came to the boys, Mum and Dad accepted that football dominated our lives. Incredibly, we all made it in the professional game. Frank began his career at Shrewsbury Town, who were managed by the British record goalscorer Arthur Rowley. He later played for QPR, Ipswich and Carlisle United. Derek initially played for Walsall before joining Wolves and won England youth honours; Kelvin also played for Walsall before moving on to Oxford and Leyton Orient; Wayne played for a number of clubs, including Wolves and Everton. Throughout our careers my parents were always at our big matches. The Clarke brothers certainly made their mark on the game!

In the 1950s, I used to watch Wolves play at Molineux. They were the best team in the Midlands and one of the top First Division sides in the country; there'd regularly be crowds of fifty or sixty thousand. Although I was only eight, I'd catch the bus on my own from Short Heath and be as safe as houses. I'd watch Wolves one week, then when they were away I'd follow Third Division Walsall. As soon as I got home from either match, I'd immediately get my boots on and practice what I'd just seen. In the summer holidays the Council used to take the football posts down on the local pitch, but we didn't play cricket, we put our jumpers down as goal posts and play from morning till night.

Although I watched Wolves on a regular basis, my team was West Bromwich Albion – but they were two bus rides away, so I never saw them that often. My hero at the time was their centre forward, Ronnie Allen. I remember him scoring twice (one a penalty) in the 1954 FA Cup final when West Brom beat Preston 3-2; Giffin scored the winning goal right at the end. When Allen was taking his penalty, West Brom's goalkeeper, Jim Sanders, refused to watch. He just stood with his back to him against one of the goal posts – he knew when West Brom had scored though by the supporters' reactions.

Other players I marvelled at were Bert Williams, Jimmy Mullen, Stanley Matthews, Stan Mortenson, Tom Finney, Nat Lofthouse, Johnny Hancocks, Billy Wright, Bert Trautmann and Len Shackleton. They were wonderful times and I couldn't wait for each game to come.

Just before I left school, there were new stars making their name. I followed the strikers, players like Bobby Charlton, Jimmy Greaves, and my favourite – Denis Law. Incredibly, later I played against all of them. Denis Law was brilliant and had everything a striker needed to be successful, but above all his quick reflexes set him apart from his competitors. What also impressed me about him was that he wouldn't hesitate to try the spectacular when nothing else seemed on. Denis was a wonderful player.

Ronnie Allen scores from the spot in the 1954 FA Cup final.

At home with Derek and Frank, 1962.

It was clear to everyone in Allan's life that, as his school days came to an end, he was only ever going to enter one profession – football. The game had dominated his every thought throughout his childhood and adolescent years, and even though only a few boys made it to the very top he was determined to make a go of it.

The first scout to approach my parents represented West Brom, my boyhood club. I was twelve at the time. I was too young to sign, but I remember him knocking on our front door and telling them he'd seen me playing for Southeast Staffordshire and wanted to sign me when I was fourteen. Nothing ever came of it. The following year, scouts from around the Midlands continually pestered my parents, but they put me under no pressure to sign for anyone. They just told me to go to the club I felt most comfortable with.

At the time I definitely lacked confidence, because not only was I short for my age, but I'd also never had a trial for England Schoolboys. The England situation always annoyed me – there's a lot of politics in schoolboy football and I knew that boys living in London got preference for national squads. I was banging in goals at all levels, but never once got offered a trial at schoolboy level.

During my last year at school, Aston Villa asked me to train with them for a week. Joe Mercer (later manager at Manchester City and Coventry) was manager and his trainer was Ray Shaw. As an incentive, Villa sent me complimentary tickets for their home matches. Two weeks before I left school I was going to sign for Villa and then, suddenly, I changed my mind. I knew the lads I'd be playing against, and I didn't think I'd do myself justice. Also, I didn't think I stood a chance of getting a taste of first-team action. I told both my parents and asked them to contact Ron Jukes, a scout at Walsall. Within days I'd joined their ground staff on £5 a week.

2

GROUND STAFF BOY
1962-1966

Allan left school in July 1962, having made the decision on where to make a name for himself. However, being given an opportunity was one thing, making it into the first team was quite another.

Walsall were in the Second Division when I joined. I was one of eight apprentices on a three-year deal trying to make it as professional players. Six worked with the groundsman during the week; I was in charge of looking after the professionals with Stan Bennett, who was into his second year on the ground staff. We'd get the training gear out for 10 a.m., clean the training and match boots, and handle the laundry. We trained on a Tuesday and Thursday evening with the amateurs – who had full-time jobs but played in emergencies if there was a spate of injuries in the reserves. Out of the apprentices only Stan Bennett, Nick Atthey, Colin Harrison and myself made it in football.

During my first season as an apprentice in 1962/63, I made just three appearances for the reserves in the Midland Intermediate League. Bill Moore was manager and generally loaned me out to a local works team on a Saturday when the reserves were playing; I wasn't very happy, but it really toughened me up. The first team, who included in their side Ken Hodgkisson, John Sharples, club skipper Albert Macpherson, George Meek, Jim Dudley and Colin 'Cannonball' Taylor – a left footer with a terrific shot – had a disastrous season, suffering relegation to the Third Division.

At the beginning of the 1963/64 season, I began to play regularly for the reserves. I'd also shot up in height and was gaining confidence with every game, but I was outgrowing my strength. I'd be at the ground by nine, home by six, and after some tea I was so tired that more often than not I'd be in bed by eight.

Allan made his Walsall debut on 3 October 1963 against Reading.

I made my debut because Jimmy O'Neil was allowed a day off to get married. I was told the news whilst cleaning the players' boots in preparation for the evening kick off. Naturally, I was delighted at this unexpected opportunity and went home to tell my family. I went back later by bus with supporters on their way to the game; it was a strange feeling knowing I was about to play and nobody knew me. I was marked by a very experienced player at that level called Spiers: he absolutely kicked chunks out of me, but I learned a lot from that match, which we drew 1-1. I played a few more

Walsall FC, 1962/63.

On holiday in Rhyl with Kelvin and Wayne, 1963.

On holiday in Margate, 1964.

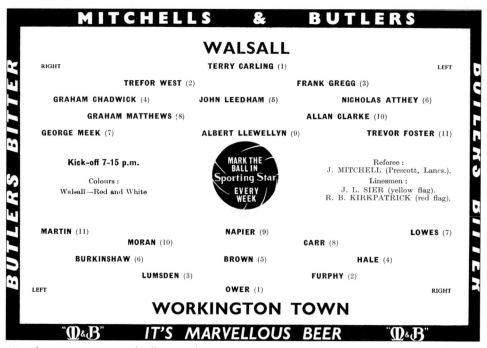

Match programme: Walsall v. Workington.

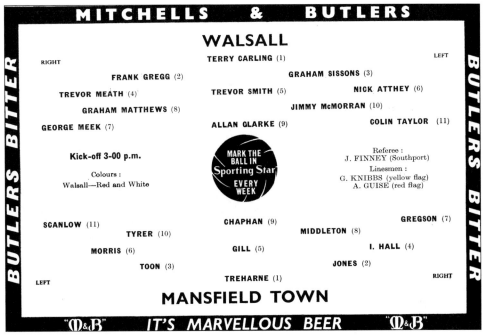

Match programme: Walsall v. Mansfield.

games during the season and was really pleased with my progress; I'd made my debut and new manager Alf Wood had included me in most of the first-team squad's training sessions.

Allan's performance got a mention in Walsall's next match programme. 'Young Allan Clarke made his debut and acquitted himself well, particularly in his headwork. More will be heard of this young man who created so many good impressions as leader of the youth team attack last season.'

The first team had a terrible start to the 1964/65 season, losing twelve matches by November. Bill Harrison took over as chairman from Ernie Thomas and his first appointment was Ray Shaw as manager.

This was a massive break for me, because I'd had coaching sessions at Aston Villa with Ray as a schoolboy. He immediately brought me back into the first team. In his first game in charge we defeated third-place Brentford 4-3. Despite being bottom of the table at Christmas, we turned results around and by our last home game of the season against Luton Town had avoided relegation. During the season we also played a prestigious friendly against Moscow Dynamo – which was an incredible experience at the time even though we were outclassed, losing the match 5-0.

I scored 23 goals and, to cap a great season, was voted the supporter's Player of the Year; Bill Harrison presented the trophy to me. Being so young I felt a bit embarrassed, but at the same time it was a tremendous honour because I knew the game

Allan receives the 1964/65 Player of the Year trophy from the chairman.

was about supporters. Throughout my career I never forgot that fans were absolutely crucial to a club's survival and an integral part of the atmosphere of a game. Also, they could make or break a young player. I was fortunate because, being so young, our fans forgave my odd mistake and were willing to be patient with me more so than with the more established stars.

Walsall may have been a small club, but the thought that went into training was as professional as anywhere I played. We had different routines to help develop our stamina, dribbling, shooting and passing. As for heading, they used to hang a ball on a pole at different heights as we ran past the halfway line of the running track. It was brilliant at improving our stretching ability from the deck. Ray Shaw organised these sessions and was the biggest influence on my Walsall career because he worked tirelessly on improving my skills. Extra training gradually developed my weaker left foot, my sharpness off the mark and my arm action while running to generate more pace.

In an interview in 1968, Shaw recalled what made Allan Clarke stand out. 'Allan has everything a goalscorer needs – height, perception, accuracy and a temperament that has always amazed me. He is confident, but not cocky. Quiet but not sulky. A lot of players play by instinct. Not Allan, he knows what to do and why.'

Being a first-team player at such a young age was fantastic. I even flew for the first time when Walsall played Southend. We rarely stayed overnight, but because of the distance Ray organised a flight from Birmingham airport. It was certainly a departure from our normal form of travel.

On a personal level I was particularly pleased for my parents who'd backed me so much. Also, I was delighted for my Auntie Celia (Mum's sister) and Uncle Harold, because they used to baby-sit for me and were Walsall fanatics. To see me make my professional debut for Walsall and begin to make a name for myself must have been wonderful for them.

Looking back, I made the right decision turning down Aston Villa, because there is no way I'd have made their first team so quickly. At the start of the 1965/66 season I had established myself in the first team and signed my first professional contract of £25 a week basic and £10 appearance money. I was getting stronger every game and was in the shop window!

By the pre-season of 1965/66, Allan was established in the squad.

Our coach Arthur Cox was just beginning his career, which took him to Newcastle and Derby County. Apart from myself, Stan Bennett had settled in at centre-half alongside Graham Sissons and Nick Atthey was running midfield. John Harris was an excellent skipper, but very few of the team made it beyond the lower leagues. One exception was my new partner in attack, the experienced striker George Kirby, who signed during the close season. I was very fortunate to have George guiding me in my

Walsall about to depart for their match at Southend.

Walsall FC, 1964/65. From left to right, back row: Cox (coach), Hodgkinson, Sissons, Bennett, Carling, Clarke, Kirby, Smith. Front row: Satchwell, Atthey, Harris, McMorran, Taylor, Gregg.

early days because you had to fight for every bit of space – and he certainly knew how to look after himself.

Allan scored the only goal of Walsall's opening fixture at Bournemouth as the team remained undefeated in eight league and cup matches. The run included a remarkable fight-back in a first round League Cup clash at home to Queens Park Rangers, which Walsall won 3-2 (4-3 on aggregate).

I scored a last-ditch winner against QPR from the penalty spot, sending Peter Springett in goal the wrong way. There was a capacity crowd that evening and, at the end of the match, supporters invaded the pitch to celebrate and carried me off shoulder high to the dressing rooms. In the next round we played West Brom in front of 41,000 spectators at the Hawthorns, but lost 3-1. However, what an experience – I wanted more of that.

Unfortunately, Walsall's League form soon dipped, even though Allan was scoring consistently. Life in the Third Division was, however, anything but mundane…

Against Millwall at the Den there was the usual intimidating atmosphere we expected; this became worse when George gave us a half-time lead. It exploded in the second half when he accidentally caught their skipper. I was twenty yards away and a fan got over the wall with a truncheon. George never saw him coming so I took him on and managed to restrain him till the police arrived. The referee threatened to

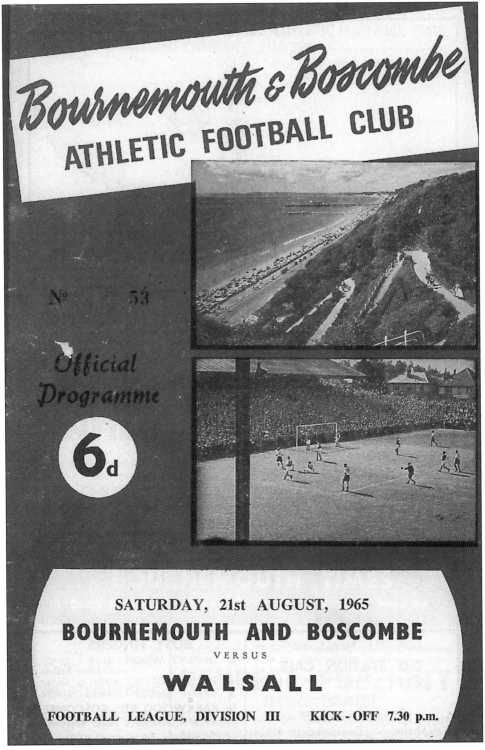

Opening game of the season, 1965/66. Allan scored the only goal of the match.

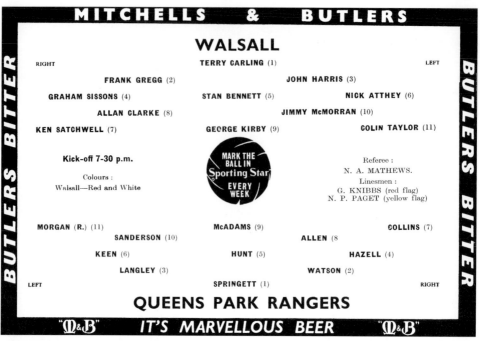

Walsall 3 QPR 2, in the League Cup first round, second leg.

Allan scores a last-minute winner to complete a famous comeback against QPR.

abandon the game but we managed to finish it. After the game our coach was pelted and we were spat at. The Den was never my favourite venue to play at.

And then there were Walsall's cup exploits.

As a kid I couldn't wait to hear the FA Cup draw, and as a player it was no different. The draw was always held the Monday after a previous round at lunchtime, and for supporters and players all over the country it became a ritual to tune in a radio to hear the draw. Like all players, a major ambition of mine was to play in an FA Cup final. I'd grown up in the 1950s watching the build-up until the presentation at the end of the match. For everyone there was always a special buzz surrounding a cup-tie, and though my preparation as a player was generally the same, the anticipation for a big cup-tie was different.

In the early rounds we defeated Swansea 6-3 and Aldershot 2-0 before the third round draw pitched us against Stoke City of the First Division. I remember Ray Shaw pouring a bottle of champagne into a football boot for the press photographers; it was a massive draw for us. I'll never forget the tie at the Victoria Ground. After the toss we swapped ends, George exchanged a few pleasantries with their centre-half Maurice Setters. Maurice asked whether he could expect a quiet afternoon, George replied, 'It's up to you!'

We lost Jimmy McMorran after fifteen minutes; there were no substitutes allowed then. From the free kick Howard Riley gave us a shock lead with a scorcher from

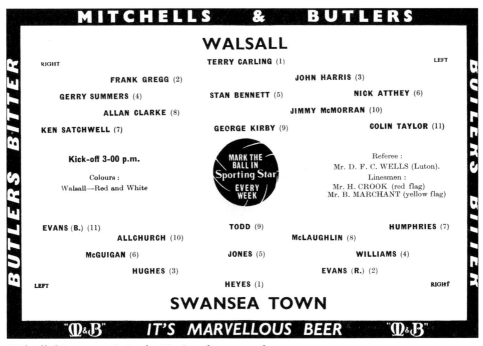

Walsall 6 Swansea 3, in the FA Cup first round.

What a draw! Stoke away in the third round of the FA Cup.

thirty yards. Stoke threw everything at us and nearly scored when Dennis Violett's shot went through the side netting into our goal. The referee initially gave a goal until the linesman rescued us. Shortly after, I received the ball and slipped past Maurice Setters. I was through but pushed the ball too far past their 'keeper Irwin. As I jumped over him, my foot caught his head and I went tumbling. The referee gave us a penalty, I sent him the wrong way: we were through.

In the fourth round we played Norwich, but luck was against us after twice taking the lead, going down 3-2. Even so, playing in the FA Cup was everything I'd expected, and knocking out one of the big guns helped me appreciate the successes that would come later in my career.

Allan Clarke played his last match for Walsall on 12 March 1966 against Grimsby, which Walsall won 1-0. He joined Fulham, aged just nineteen, later that month for a club record fee of £37,500.

Our cup run naturally made the national papers and, for me, the exposure was doing my career no harm at all. I was used to my name appearing in the football snippets of the Sunday papers, speculating what club may be interested in me. Personally, I would have loved Aston Villa, Wolves or West Brom to come in, but it didn't happen. However, one club had made enquiries about me all season, Fulham. Naturally this was flattering, but Vic Buckingham's offers were continually rejected, the highest being £20,000.

On transfer deadline day Ray Shaw called me into his office before training and informed me that Fulham had made another bid, which the club had accepted. Was I interested? Of course I was – this was an opportunity to join a First Division club. I was told to go home for lunch and return to Fellows Park in the afternoon for talks.

When I returned I had to wait a while, because Ray's car had broken down. I had been suffering from an ankle injury, so went to the treatment room and had a rest on the treatment table. I fell asleep. Ray Shaw woke me and told me that Vic Buckingham had finally arrived. I met him in the boardroom and quickly realised he thought I was so desperate to play in Division One that I'd sign for next to nothing. I refused his terms. My ambition was to play in the top league, but I was determined to get a fair deal. After four hours he finally relented. I signed for £50 a week and a signing on bonus. At nineteen, I had made it into top-flight football, but I had to prove I could do it.

3

COTTAGE DAYS
1966-1968

In March 1966 Allan began life in the top flight of the Football League.

Twenty-four hours after signing for Fulham, I travelled down to London by train and moved into digs five minutes from Craven Cottage. Fulham had signed me as a replacement for Rodney Marsh, whose individual style was a favourite with supporters but not the manager. Rodney had joined QPR for a ridiculously low fee of £15,000, but that was not my concern; I was about to meet my new team-mates, many being household names. Johnny Haynes had captained England, George Cohen was England's regular right-back, then there was Bobby Robson, Tony Mercado, Les Barrett and Graham Leggatt. I was delighted.

Fulham was a really friendly club; their chairman was the comedian Tommy Trinder. I was a bit in awe the first time I met this comic legend – after all, I'd only seen him performing on Sunday Night at the London Palladium *on television. He was a lovely man and was forever taking the mick out of my Black Country accent.*

At the time Fulham were involved in a relegation battle. A few weeks before Allan joined they were adrift at the bottom of the table by five points, but by the time Allan had made his debut on 8 April 1966, five straight victories had been chalked up.

When I joined Fulham I was still carrying an ankle injury, so watched them defeat Sunderland and West Ham – I was impressed. I began training and was made substitute for the home game against Leeds United. Johnny Haynes went off injured, so I finally made my First Division debut. We were trailing by two goals and eventually lost 3-1. With Johnny out I was given a run in the first team, playing the link role. I made my first full appearance in a rearranged fixture at Elland Road. We were really fired up and avenged our home defeat thanks to a great goal from Mark 'Pancho' Pearson.

What I mainly recall about these games was the step-up in ability playing against the likes of Bremner, Charlton, Hunter and Giles – names I'd just heard of before, and I was impressed: they were real class. These games were also the first time Don Revie had seen me and he told me years later that he made a mental note of my play, and especially how I wasn't afraid to mix it!

I moved into digs with Percy Sell, who introduced me to local people and generally helped me settle in the area. By the Easter programme, Johnny Haynes was back in the side and I moved into attack. We picked up two away victories, the first proving

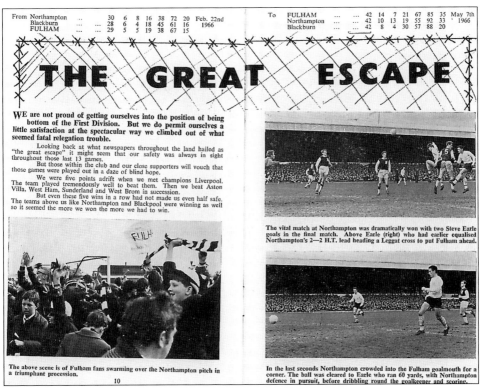

From Northampton	..	30	6	8	16	38	72	20	Feb. 22nd	To	FULHAM	...	...	42	14	7	21	67	85	35	May 7th
Blackburn	...	28	6	4	18	45	61	16	1966		Northampton	...	...	42	10	13	19	55	92	33	1966
FULHAM	...	29	5	5	19	38	67	15			Blackburn	...	...	42	8	4	30	57	88	20	

THE GREAT ESCAPE

WE are not proud of getting ourselves into the position of being bottom of the First Division. But we do permit ourselves a little satisfaction at the spectacular way we climbed out of what seemed fatal relegation trouble.

Looking back at what newspapers throughout the land hailed as "the great escape" it might seem that our safety was always in sight throughout those last 13 games.

But those within the club and our close supporters will vouch that those games were played out in a daze of blind hope.

We were five points adrift when we met champions Liverpool. The team played tremendously well to beat them. Then we beat Aston Villa, West Ham, Sunderland and West Brom in succession.

But even these five wins in a row had not made us even half safe. The teams above us like Northampton and Blackpool were winning as well so it seemed the more we won the more we had to win.

The vital match at Northampton was dramatically won with two Steve Earle goals in the final match. Above Earle (right) who had earlier equalised Northampton's 2—2 H.T. lead heading a Leggat cross to put Fulham ahead.

The above scene is of Fulham fans swarming over the Northampton pitch in a triumphant procession.

10

In the last seconds Northampton crowded into the Fulham goalmouth for a corner. The ball was cleared to Earle who ran 60 yards, with Northampton defence in pursuit, before dribbling round the goalkeeper and scoring.

Fulham survive the drop!

crucial at our relegation rivals, Northampton, where a Steve Earle hat-trick in our 4-2 win guaranteed our safety. The feeling in the dressing room was one of pure relief.

Three days later, we won 2-1 at Nottingham Forest. At the match was my fiancée, Margaret, who lived in Stapleford near Nottingham. Life could not have been more hectic, because in addition to moving to London we were due to get married on her birthday, 11 June 1966, which clashed with Fulham's close season tour to the Far East. I resolved this particular issue during my negotiations with Vic Buckingham, agreeing to play the first four games of the tour before returning home for our big day.

We drew our remaining two fixtures of the campaign at home to Stoke City and at Newcastle United. The Stoke match in particular was memorable for me because I grabbed my first goal for Fulham.

Allan went with Fulham on their post-season tour to the Far East. George Cohen missed the tour because he was preparing for the 1966 World Cup with England, but all the other players travelled, including some of the younger members of the squad similar in age to Allan: Steve Earle, Les Barrett and John Dempsey.

The tournament was a tremendous experience, especially adapting to the humid and sticky conditions that were so different to home. After playing in Hong Kong,

Fulham depart for their post-season tour to the Far East.

Allan and Margaret on their wedding day.

Singapore and Kuala Lumpur, I flew home from Penang via Singapore for my wedding to Margaret two days later. We chose not to have a honeymoon because we wanted to get settled into the area before pre-season training started. There was also the small matter of watching the 1966 World Cup finals during a hectic summer.

Fulham got off to a terrible start in 1966/67, winning just two out of their opening fifteen matches. By far their best performance in this torrid time was a 2-2 draw with defending champions Liverpool.

Scoring on any occasion at Anfield was special, so to score twice meant an awful lot to me. The second was a bit special and is still one of my favourites. It was opposite the Kop end. I picked the ball up just inside their half and went on a mazy run past a number of players before slipping it past Tommy Lawrence in goal. After the game, Bill Shankly said it was one of the finest goals he'd ever seen at Anfield – which was some compliment.

Fulham suddenly began to pull their season round with a run that included seven victories in nine games, but they could not keep the momentum going, winning just two more games all season. Fortunately, the purple patch they'd had was sufficient to

Fulham team group, 1966/67.

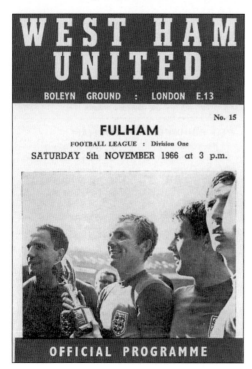

Match programme for West Ham v. Fulham. Note the 1966 World Cup heroes George Cohen, Bobby Moore and Geoff Hurst on the cover.

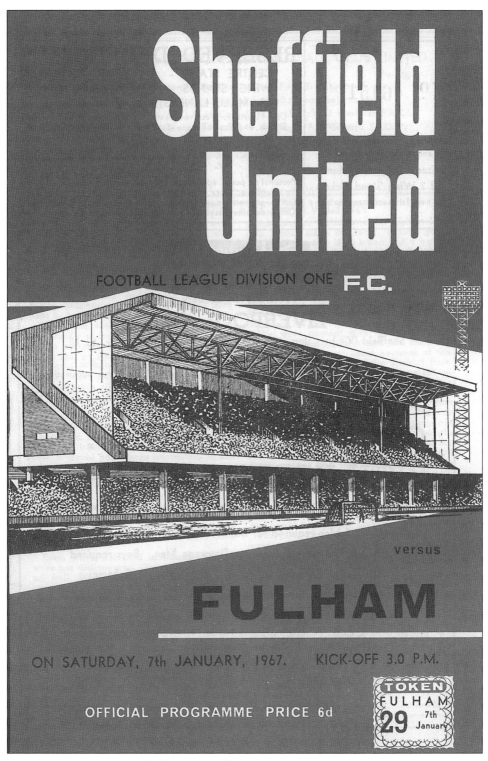

Match programme: Sheffield Utd. v. Fulham.

Another goal, this time at St James Park.

Scrapping for possession at White Hart Lane.

avoid relegation, but it was very close. It had been a great season for Allan, with opposing defenders and Sir Alf Ramsey being quick to note his success.

Although Fulham struggled for consistency, I was really pleased with my own form during my first season in the First Division. Not only did I play in every League match, but I bagged 29 goals in all competitions, the highlight being my hat-trick at home to Newcastle in a 5-1 win.

Unfortunately, my goals made me a marked man. I was involved in a brawl during Fulham's clash with Tottenham that resulted in Fred Callaghan and Terry Venables being dismissed in February 1967, then towards the end of the season I was sent off for the first time in my career, along with Arsenal's Ian Ure, at Craven Cottage.

It was an end-of-season match where all that mattered to supporters was local pride. The game was ill-tempered from the start. Terry Neil was marking me particularly tight, and the referee was giving me no protection from a number of hard challenges. I was not happy. Just before half time I was hacked down for the umpteenth time for what seemed a certain penalty; the referee gave a free kick. Then Ian Ure fouled me from the free kick – we collided in mid-air – and I landed on top of him. There was an almighty brawl, where the worst offence was pushing and shoving as every player seemed to get involved, trying to act as peacemakers. The referee, Mr Osborne, sent us both off for fighting! I was livid and felt hard done by. I received a week's suspension and a £25 fine, Ian Ure's fine was double mine.

In the early part of the season, Alf Ramsey didn't pick me for his first under-23 squad of the season to play Wales. I was disappointed. Peter Osgood of Chelsea was ahead of me, but he broke a leg at Blackpool. The next day, Vic Buckingham informed me that Alf wanted me in his squad – it wasn't the best of circumstances to win my first international call up, but I was determined to take my chance. Alf managed the Under-23 side, and his trainers were Les Cocker and Harold Shepardson. I loved playing for Alf Ramsey: he respected his players and was an absolute gentleman. You could not help but be impressed immediately and you always wanted to play well for him.

We trained at Wolves' Castle Croft training ground on the Tuesday afternoon. That evening we went to Fellows Park to see Walsall play Gillingham. It was very strange watching the match from the directors' box, but I really enjoyed going back to the club that had given me my first chance in football.

> The home side for the England *v.* Wales under-23 international: Farmer (Stoke), Thomson (Wolves, captain), Knowles (Tottenham), Hollins (Chelsea), Stephenson (Crystal Palace), Harris (Chelsea), Coates (Burnley), Sammels (Arsenal), Clarke (Fulham), Ford (Sheffield Wednesday), Sissons (West Ham).

All my family were there to see me score four goals on my international debut as England crushed Wales 8-0. Although Wales were very poor, Alf saw what I could do and that was important for me.

With Walsall chairman Bill Harrison and England manager Sir Alf Ramsey after his England under-23 debut.

The papers were full of praise. Bernard Joy of *The Evening Standard* wrote, 'The label "Mexico 1970" can be pinned on Fulham centre forward Allan Clarke. Against Wales, Clarke was outstanding, holding the attack together with nonchalant ease and using deadly finishing to score four goals.' David Miller in the *Sunday Telegraph* was equally enthusiastic about Allan: 'Like the headwaiter of a five-star hotel, Clarke is everywhere without ever being ostentatious. He has the virtue not characteristic of many of our leading players, elegance, and the quality that usually distinguishes outstanding wing-halves rather than forwards, of doing everything at his own, often seemingly leisurely pace. Here is a player to woo an outside world not over-impressed with the "revival" of English soccer.'

In March 1967 I was chosen to play for the Football League against the Scottish League at Hampden Park. I managed to score two of our goals in a 3-0 win. This was the first time I'd played with the likes of Moore, Hurst and Greaves, and I certainly enjoyed it.

> Football League *v.* Scottish League: Bonetti (Chelsea), Badger (Sheffield United), Newton (Blackburn), Hollins (Chelsea), Labone (Everton), Moore (West Ham, captain), Callaghan (Liverpool), Greaves (Tottenham), Clarke (Fulham), Hurst (West Ham), Thompson (Liverpool).

Peter Lorenzo of *The Sun* wrote, 'Clarke, at home with England's 4-3-3 as much as he is with his club formation, has a most impressive Football League debut. His two splendidly taken goals were fine reward for his endeavour. Here is a player, not yet twenty-one, who impresses with his maturity and effective nonchalant approach to big time occasions.' Allan's two-goal performance for Young England against England at Highbury in a 5-0 win brought more national headlines, including the statement 'This is Sir Alf's chance to freshen his jaded World Champions … Allan Clarke is ready to lead England.'

Alan Hoby of the *Sunday Express* wrote, 'For the first time since England won the World Cup, an unusual challenger of potential greatness is in line for the vital No. 9 spot in the national team. He is Allan Clarke, a fluent, elastic-limbed young pulse-raiser from Fulham, who showed his quality when he scored two penalty goals and hit the post twice in Young England's whipping of England at Highbury.'

By the end of the season I'd helped the under-23s defeat Austria 3-0 at Hull before going with the squad on a post-season tour of Greece, Bulgaria and Turkey. Bill Nicholson took charge of the tour and it was quite an experience. I played in all three games. We began by drawing against Greece 0-0, then the most controversial match took place in Sofia and turned into a brawl, due to cynical tactics by the Bulgarians. The match ended 1-1, but I still remember a right uppercut from Bulgarian defender Christakiev that nearly knocked me out. We finished the tour with a 3-0 win in Ankara, when I managed to score our third goal.

> The England under-23 *v.* Turkey under-23 side: Montgomery (Sunderland), Wright (Everton), Knowles (Tottenham), Hurst (Everton), Mobley (Sheffield Wednesday, captain), Newton (Nottingham Forest), Coates (Burnley), Harvey (Everton), Clarke (Fulham), O'Rourke (Middlesborough), Sammels (Arsenal).

Allan Clarke had made people sit up and notice his talents in his first season at Fulham. At the tender age of twenty he had scored goals galore, been sent off for brawling, represented his country and the Football League, and been praised and lambasted in equal measure. Critics had labelled him lazy, greedy, egotistical, and uncontrollable in one breath, then the great hope and a breath of fresh air for England in the next. He got on with many of the established stars, but clashed with management as well. Life was anything but dull.

I got on particularly well with George Cohen, who was a very gifted defender and the model professional footballer. George was skipper of the side and helped Margaret and I settle into our new surroundings. George was also a tremendous influence on

Allan Clarke, 1967/68.

England Under-23s take a break from training in Greece. From left to right, back row: Harvey, Springett, Montgomery, Husband, Knowles, Winfield, Hurst, Sibley. Front row: Barrett, Mobly, O'Rourke, Clarke, Sammels, Coates, Newton.

England and Greece line up before their Under-23 clash. From left to right. Mobly, Knowles, Montgomery, Husband, Harvey, Barrett, Coates, Sammels, Winfield, Hurst, Clarke.

me in developing good habits. We used to talk for hours about everything to do with the game, and most Sundays he would come round to help me analyse how I could improve my game. George was a very popular captain at Fulham: there was no yelling or bawling, just words of encouragement all the time. You never took offence when George had a quiet word about something you were doing wrong. Even when he was out injured he'd watch us play and advise us. He was such a calming influence.

Then there was the 'King', Johnny Haynes, the first £100-a-week footballer. Johnny was the star of the team. He played for England at every level and captained them. As a kid I saw him play for Fulham at Wolves – his distribution was masterful. I also remember seeing him play for England at Wembley on television. Johnny was near the end of his career, but there was still an aura about him and the fans worshipped him. At times we didn't get on – part of it was my fault because I refused to bow to his fame and reputation, other times it was his because I was the young upstart and had to know my place.

Johnny Haynes was a great player though, one of the best I ever took the field with. He was a perfectionist and the playmaker of the side. His satisfaction was making a goal rather than scoring one. As a striker, when you made a run you wanted a ball to be played into you, with Johnny I knew his cross would be inch perfect – all I had to do was put the ball in the net. I know that's easier said than done, but his passes made my job much easier. I loved playing with him as the linkman behind me; he made me a lot of goals.

The most difficult aspect to life at Fulham was my relationship with Vic

Fulham's international stars, August 1967. George Cohen (left) *and Johnny Haynes* (right)

WHAT A GAME !

2—2   2—2   2—2   2—2   2—2   2—2

The fact that we were twice in the lead against Manchester United helped to create the tension and excitement in our Easter Monday game. Allan Clarke (left) scored our first in the 18th minute. We were given a free kick for a foul on Pearson. Haynes hit it perfectly into the goalmouth and Clarke beat Foulkes in the air to score with a header.

Our second goal (below) came at the end of what was probably the best move of the season. A lot of the credit must go to George Cohen. Cohen had hit the upright with a tremendous shot. The ball rebounded over his head and straight to the feet of United left winger Aston. The winger raced down the empty field with Cohen in hot pursuit and the Fulham skipper saved a nasty situation by harrassing Aston into a poor cross. The ball was whipped down the right wing to Haynes (centre) who passed perfectly across to Pearson (left through net) who passed equally accurately to Barrett (right) whose shot almost burst through the top of the net.

The whole movement was executed so quickly and cleverly that United didn't know what hit them. But like the great side they are United were soon hitting back and with six minutes to go Nobby Stiles beat Macedo to a Charlton cross to score the equaliser which no-one could begrudge them.

(Photos by Ken Coton)

Action from Fulham's 2-2 draw at Manchester Utd.

41

Buckingham. There was no question that he was a fine coach with a flair for organisation in training, but as a man-manager we clashed. His attitude at times amazed me: a number of times he came into our dressing room and just read a newspaper saying nothing. Tony Mercado once stood up and started singing the song 'Good morning, Good morning …' – he never flinched.

During the season we had a terrific result at League leaders Manchester United. I scored one of our goals in a 2-2 draw. The players were really pleased with themselves, but Vic thought we should have done better. I had a stand-up argument, telling him how unreasonable he was.

Pre-season I was entitled to new terms but we couldn't agree. I handed in a transfer request, which Vic refused. He told me I could carry on handing in requests, he'd just tear them up. I became more determined. The week before the opening game of the 1967/68 campaign he finally agreed to my request of £70 per week – not an exceptional demand considering the number of goals I had scored for Fulham. I asked him why he'd argued for so long. He told me if I'd re-signed for less Fulham's directors would have been delighted with him. I couldn't believe how petty Fulham had been;

SHEFFIELD WEDNESDAY BLUE AND WHITE		FULHAM WHITE SHIRTS, BLACK SHORTS
1. SPRINGETT, Peter	Referee : T. A. PALLISTER, Peterlee.	1. SEYMOUR, Ian
2. QUINN, John		2. COHEN, George
3. MEGSON, Don		3. DEMPSEY, John
4. MOBLEY, Vic.		4. BROWN, Stan
5. ELLIS, Sam		5. NICHOLS, Brian
6. YOUNG, Gerry		6. CONWAY, Jimmy
7. USHER, Brian		7. PEARSON, Mark
8. McCALLIOG, Jim		8. BARRETT, Les.
9. RITCHIE, John	Linesmen :	9. RYAN, John
10. FANTHAM, John	F. ELLIS, Halifax (red flag) ;	10. CLARKE, Allan
11. FORD, David	J. B. GOGGINS, Manchester (yellow flag).	11. PARMENTER, Tony
Sub.:...........................		Sub.:...........................

OZZIE OWL WELCOMES FULHAM

" Let's put on a good show Tommy "

Match programme: Sheffield Wednesday v. Fulham.

Allan on the attack at Hillsborough.

Match action from Fulham's game with West Brom.

my goals had kept them up, which was worth an awful lot more than the increase I was after. Nevertheless, I looked forward to the new campaign.

Fulham got off to another terrible start in 1967/68 and failed to find any consistency at all, apart from three successive victories in November 1967. Allan got a severe warning in his opening game of the season at Sunderland and the FA suspended him for two weeks after he had been booked three times. The media had a field-day. Norman Giller of the *Daily Express* wrote 'Allan Clarke is fighting a battle with himself to control a temper that is threatening to overshadow his vast talent. Clarke – just twenty-one, tall, full of fire – is exactly the type of sharp-shooting forward England need to help hang on to the World Cup in Mexico in 1970. But there is a chance that his quick temper could trip him up before he can clinch a place in the England attack.'

In a frank interview with Giller, Allan admitted,

'I've got a temper that gets me into trouble. I know that I should control it, but that's easier said than done. I am an eager player and want to be where the action is, and when you are up against two or three defenders who are determined to stop you at any cost then things are liable to happen in the heat of the moment. You can imagine how hard it is for me to stay cool and calm when somebody is kicking away at my legs, and now I've got a reputation for banging in goals some defenders try to sort me out more than they used to. It makes things very difficult.'

Allan knew he had to change. His problems apart, Fulham changed manager mid-term, Bobby Robson succeeding Vic Buckingham. However there was to be no 'great escape' this time as Fulham remained in the bottom two. Towards the end of the season, Bobby Robson had a meeting with Allan.

I respected Bobby Robson enormously and he knew how to put things over to players. He presented himself well and had a great understanding of the game. When Bobby took over not all the players were happy, the older players felt a bit jealous and threatened, but I was delighted because he gave great advice. Even though we were virtually down he bucked us up, and we gave our all, even in a desperate situation. Relegation was inevitable and he had to start planning ahead. He didn't want me to leave but realised I'd want to stay in the First Division and would not stand in my way. Also, my fee would enable him to rebuild. Bobby felt I was now one of the best young strikers around and would demand a high transfer fee. He told me to hold out for similar wages.

Manchester United made the first bid, a British record of £150,000.

I met Matt Busby and Jimmy Murphy at Kings Cross Station. We got in a taxi and Matt told the driver to drive around London while we chatted. Matt told me he thought they would win the title that year and hopefully the European Cup. I agreed to join in the close season. At the end of the campaign it was of little consolation that I finished top-

VOL 1   NO 4
MARCH 1968

PRICE
1/-

FULHAM F.C.
SUPPORTERS CLUB
OFFICIAL MAGAZINE

Allan introduces himself to Billy Bremner!

What a win! Fulham 4 Burnley 3.

Allan scores a consolation goal against champions elect, Manchester City.

What a hammering! West Ham 7 Fulham 2.

scorer again with 27 goals. The season was summed up by a number of heavy defeats, the worst of them a 7-2 drubbing at West Ham. I felt really sorry for Tommy Trinder, who loved the club so much, but I knew it was time to move on.

On the eve of the Cup final I was due to play for England v. Young England at Highbury. Bobby informed me that Leicester had also bid £150,000 and their chairman would be at the game, would I meet him at the end of the match in the reception area at the ground? I agreed. After our 4-1 defeat I went to meet him as arranged. After an hour I got fed up and went home. At midnight the phone went; it was Leicester's chairman explaining why he'd missed me and asking if he could get a taxi to my home from his Paddington hotel. When he arrived we chatted for a while and I agreed to meet Leicester's manager, Matt Gillies, the next day. Within minutes of talking to Matt I wanted to play for him and signed a three-year contract. I rang Matt Busby to tell him my decision. He was disappointed, but wished me well. Next day Don Revie rang, he told me he was coming in for me!

Looking back people find it astonishing I turned down the chance to sign for Manchester United, however, I knew it was the right decision. They had some fantastic players, but within the game people knew Charlton, Law and Best were at their peak and would soon need replacing. As it happens, Manchester United won nothing for a decade whereas I had the most successful period of my career.

To put Allan's transfer fee in perspective, in 1968 a detached house or a Rolls Royce cost £5,000; £150,000 was a colossal amount of money, smashing the previous record of

£125,000 that Tottenham paid Southampton for Martin Chivers.

The actual fee didn't bother me – that was between the clubs – but it did place me firmly in the spotlight. I was continually talked about, written about, pictured, and instantly criticised for the slightest thing and that was hard to handle at times. On the field I was now the most expensive footballer in Britain and defenders already had me down as a marked man because I scored regularly. I knew it would not get easier. Fortunately, I could handle myself. Although I was no worse than other strikers of my era, I knew I had to control my aggression because I'd be tackled harder and provoked continually.

4

LUCKLESS LEICESTER
1968/69

Allan's time at Leicester City was problematic throughout. He had joined because of Matt Gillies' persuasive arguments about the team's potential, with the likes of Peter Shilton, Graham Cross, David Gibson, Andy Lockhead and David Nish. Unfortunately, poor results and off-the-field turmoil made for an uneasy twelve months.

I scored in our opening game, a 1-1 draw at QPR. Match of the Day was there, one of the reasons being that Frank (my brother) and myself were on opposing sides. At the end, commentator David Coleman interviewed us together. I then struck a hat-trick over defending champions Manchester City for our first win of the season. Unfortunately, we soon found points really hard to come by.

In October 1968 Matt made me captain after Willie Bell was injured. I was reluctant to take it because I felt a striker was too far removed from the play as a whole. Nevertheless, I accepted the role. Against Burnley I was dismissed for retaliation after their skipper, Colin Waldron, caught me with a bad challenge. I'm not condoning what I did, but I was a fiery character and opponents took advantage.

A few weeks later we lost 7-1 at Everton. The Board sacked Matt Gillies' right-hand man, Bert Johnson, and Matt resigned in protest. I couldn't believe it. I went round to Matt's house with Willie Bell to try and change his mind, but he stuck to his principles. Frank O'Farrell replaced him.

I never got on with Frank from the start. I missed his first game in charge because I was still serving the suspension for my sending off and David Nish took over the captaincy. After regaining fitness I assumed the captaincy would revert to me, but before the next match Frank announced David would carry on. I didn't mind that particularly, but I was very upset by the manner in which it was done.

Leicester were really struggling in the League, but made superb progress in the FA Cup.

In the third round we defeated Barnsley. What I remember most about the tie was a goal I scored that wasn't given. I volleyed a great strike from twelve yards, which struck the stanchion but bounced straight out again. I raised my arm to signal a goal, but Jack Taylor waved play on – he'd missed it! After defeating Millwall we drew Liverpool at home, which was a cracking tie for us. At Filbert Street we struggled to break them down, but in the replay we frustrated them and scored on the break through Andy Lockhead. Another 1-0 victory was sufficient to defeat Mansfield in the quarter finals.

In the semi-finals we faced the cup holders, West Brom, who were clear favourites

Leicester City FC: 1968/69. From left to right, back row: Fern, Cross, Roberts, Gibson. Middle row: Sjoberg, Stringfellow, Shilton, Woollett, Mackleworth, Bell, Clarke. Front row: Rodrigues, Nish, Tewley, Hutchins, Potts, Manley, Glover.

David Coleman interviews Frank and Allan for Match of the Day.

PICTURE RECORD OF A GREAT OCCASION

A hat trick is a land mark in any career and we rated Allan Clarke's treble against Manchester City worthy of a permanent record. The top picture—goal number 1—shows Clarke having followed through to the posts. Goal number 2 has been netted by the lone Clarke from Gibson's pass and in the bottom picture the scorer has just completed his turn after driving home that fine left footer.   *Neville Chadwick Photography*

Allan's hat-trick against Manchester City.

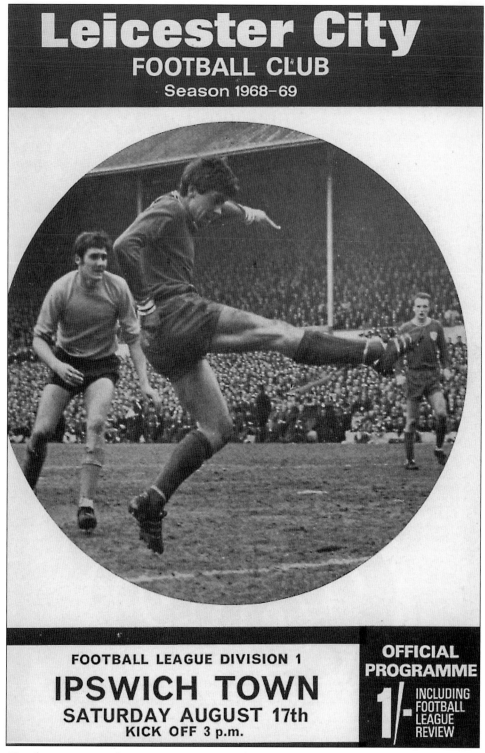

Match programme from Leicester v. Ipswich.

Allan and Peter Shilton keep West Bromwich at bay in their semi-final clash.

because they were a better team man-for-man. We hustled and fought for every ball, then a few minutes from time struck. One of their centre-halves, John Kaye, hoofed the ball clear; it ballooned high in the air and, as it came down, I was lurking outside the box and I knew I was going to volley it. Fortunately, West Brom's defenders failed to close me down and as it dropped I caught it nicely. It fitted perfectly. I went off injured just before the end and was in the dressing room when the final whistle went, but I was delighted. I was in my first FA Cup final.

Reaching Wembley was a fantastic achievement. In the final we would face Manchester City, who had a cracking side. Their players were all household names and their front five – Mike Summerbee, Colin Bell, Francis Lee, Neil Young and Tony Coleman – was arguably the best around.

A week before the cup final I scored twice in the Under-23s' 4-0 win over Portugal. My final game for the Under-23s earned me a place on England's South American trip, instead of the Under-23 tour. My critics started to believe in me!

England Under-23 *v.* Portugal Under-23: Shilton (Leicester), Smith (Sheffield Wednesday), Pardoe (Manchester City), Doyle (Manchester City), Booth (Manchester City), Sadler (Manchester United), Coates

Wembley, here I come!

That's our boys! Allan's proud parents with their sons Frank (QPR kit), Allan, Derek (Wolves kit), Kelvin (QPR kit) and Wayne (Leeds kit). All five Clarke brothers played professional football and they are shown here in 1969.

Leicester City: 1969 FA Cup final squad. From left to right, back row: Fern, Sjoberg, Shilton, Roberts, Cross, Lochhead, Clarke. Front row: Gibson, Rodrigues, Nish, Glover.

(Burnley), Robson (Newcastle), Clarke (Leicester), Evans (Liverpool), Sissons (West Ham).

The Sun reported, 'Allan Clarke, Britain's most expensive footballer who would no doubt swap his Leicester Cup final ticket allocation for a World Cup place in Mexico, gave two good reasons last night why he could be there. He scored two goals and also fired a broadside at the critics who accuse him of not working hard enough in a team formation.'

For the final, Frank O'Farrell changed our formation, picking me to play in midfield after I'd played striker all season. I still have no idea why he played me in that role. There are two people you never play out of position, a goalkeeper and a striker. It was a crazy decision. During the build-up to the match players who had experienced a Cup final before told me to take as much of the day in as I could because it would fly by – and it did. We played really well and were a little unfortunate to lose 1-0. Nevertheless, I really enjoyed the occasion and was delighted to be voted Man of the Match.

Most soccer pundits gave Leicester great reviews. *The Observer's* Hugh McIlvanney wrote. 'If Manchester take credit for their adherence to the Mercer-Allison creed of class first, last and always, Leicester can look back with pride to an afternoon on which they rose far above the standards that have dragged them sadly close to relegation. In

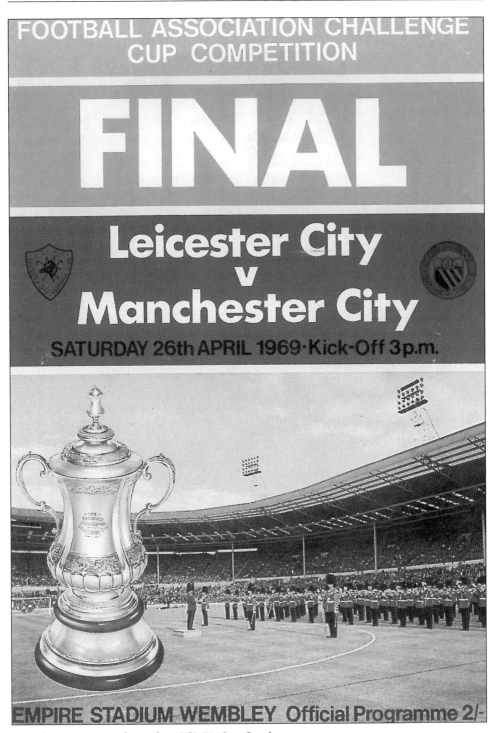

Match programme from the 1969 FA Cup final.

Leicester on the attack at Wembley.

a real sense, they made the match what it was, for it was their willingness to forgo any thought of a negative approach that gave us a thrillingly open contest.'

> Manchester City *v.* Leicester City, 1969 FA Cup final.
> *Manchester City*: Dowd, Book (captain), Pardoe, Doyle, Booth, Oakes, Summerbee, Bell, Lee, Young, Coleman, Connor (substitute).
> *Leicester City*: Shilton, Rodrigues, Nish (captain), Roberts, Woolett, Cross, Fern, Gibson, Lockhead, Clarke, Glover, Manley (substitute).

After their Cup final defeat, Leicester played their final League games of the season. Five wins since the turn of the year meant only a victory in their last game at Manchester United would save them from relegation.

Normally I would have stayed overnight to prepare, but leading up to the game Margaret was in hospital and came out a couple of days before the game. I asked Frank if I could travel up on the morning of the game because I needed to help with our baby daughter, but he refused. After a long argument I managed to get a relative to help out at home. I travelled with the team, but I knew my days at Leicester were over. Frank told me before the match Leicester were prepared to let me go whatever the result, and asked me to do my best. I made a goal to put us ahead, but we lost the

Margaret and Allan after being presented with the Man of the Match award.

game 3-2 and were relegated.

The final weeks of the season had been very stressful off the field and it was no secret at the time that I had been unhappy at Leicester since Matt Gillies left. There was a lot of speculation in the media of various clubs coming in for me, but that would have to wait as I jetted off for England's tour of South America in preparation for the 1970 World Cup. We drew our first match with Mexico in Mexico City before moving on to Guadalajara, where I played in an England XI that defeated a Mexico XI 4-0. Apart from scoring two goals, I was involved in a bizarre incident that saw Alan Mullery sent off when he argued with the referee after I'd been fouled.

England XI *v.* Mexico XI: Shilton (Leicester), Wright (Everton), McNab (Arsenal), Harvey (Everton), Charlton J. (Leeds), Moore (West Ham,

Leicester City
FOOTBALL CLUB
Season 1968–69

FOOTBALL LEAGUE DIVISION 1
TOTTENHAM HOTSPUR
**TUESDAY, 29th APRIL
KICK-OFF 7.30 p.m.**

OFFICIAL PROGRAMME

6d

After the cup final it's back to League action against Tottenham.

Allan and Bobby Moore at an England training session.

captain), Ball (Everton), Clarke (Leicester), Astle (West Brom), Bell (Manchester City), Peters (West Ham). Substitutes: Mullery (Tottenham, for Ball), Charlton R. (Manchester United, for Peters). Full international caps were not awarded for this game.

We defeated Uruguay 2-1 in Montevideo, before jetting off to Rio de Janeiro to face Brazil in our final match of the tour. At the time, Pele was just 30 short of 1,000 first-class goals, so I was looking forward to seeing the world's greatest footballer at close quarters. I wasn't disappointed. We lost the game 2-1 in front of 160,000 spectators at the famous Maracana stadium. It had been a great trip and I knew I was well placed to be in the final squad for the World Cup, which was now just twelve months away.

5

TREBLE CHANCE
1969/70

When Allan got back from Brazil, Leicester informed him they had accepted a new British record bid of £165,000 from Leeds United.

I believed in my own ability. I was single-minded and wanted to be the best. Don Revie and Manny Cussins came round to my home to sort out terms. Don asked what wages I wanted, I told him I would like £10 a week more than I was on at Leicester. He refused and told me all his players were on the same wage. Who was I to disbelieve him?

At the same time I was informed I wasn't getting my cut of the players' pool from the Cup final. I was not happy. I'd contributed more than anyone else had and explained that I could not contribute fees for newspaper articles and magazine interviews organised by my literary agent Ernest Hecht. The letter summed up my problems at Leicester. They were not a huge club with lots of stars, and there was definitely resentment by some players that I was asked to make the most personal appearances. I was glad to get away. Leicester also insisted I'd asked for a transfer, so withheld my signing-on fee. I disputed this and the matter went to an FA tribunal. I lost the case and got a slating in the press. Bad press was by now something I was used to.

At Fulham and Leicester we lost more than we won and I felt terrible after a defeat. Unfortunately, some of my colleagues didn't display the same disappointment as me so I was accused of being a 'loner'. Avoiding relegation and a good cup run was not sufficient for me; I wanted to be challenging for trophies all the time because that would help my international aspirations. At the end of my first season at Leeds, a reporter rang me looking for a story, I had nothing to say – I always had something to say before, the 'loner' stories had finally stopped!

I was also called 'greedy', which upset me. Of course terms were important, but my motives for moving were always football-related, I simply wanted to better myself. Then there was the 'lazy' tag. I would be the first to admit that I never chased every lost cause – that wasn't my game – but my critics should have seen me in the dressing room after a match: I was always shattered. Throughout a game the demands on a striker were enormous as you were constantly searching for openings. I did have a temper though and it was my nature to argue. I realised I had to work on my discipline and began to get on top of it after joining Leeds, but never really mastered it. My only excuse was that I was desperate to win.

Leeds United, August 1969. From left to right, back row: Revie (manager), Reaney, Hunter, Belfitt, Gray. Middle row: O'Grady, Charlton, Sprake, Harvey, Jones, Madeley. Front row: Clarke, Cooper, Hibbitt, Bremner, Giles, Bates.

Not all articles were critical though. One of the most amusing appeared in the *Daily Express* under the heading, 'What Makes Allan Clarke a £350,000 Footballer'. David Turner produced a sketch of Allan with arrows pointing to various parts of his body. Norman Giller diagnosed why four clubs had paid £350,000 in total for his services. An arrow pointed to Allan's head: '6ft 1in tall. Commanding in the air. Vision perfect. Alert football brain. Acts exceptionally quickly in decisive situations.' An arrow pointed to Allan's chest: 'Chest 38in (normal), 41in (expanded). Adept at chesting the ball down. Likes to turn and shoot in one movement.' An arrow pointed to Allan's hips: 'Waist 30in, Allows for agility and fast swivel in a confined space. Quick acceleration and deceptive change of pace. Long, loping stride takes him through 100 yards in 10.2 secs.' An arrow pointed to Allan's stomach: 'Weight 10st 4lb. Evenly distributed. Shoots powerfully and accurately with either foot. Favours the right. Wears size 8 boots and passes precisely up to distances of 60 yards.'

Don Revie was asked many times why he purchased Allan Clarke. His views were documented in his foreword for Allan's coaching book *Soccer: How to become a Champion*. It is clear Revie was impressed from the first time he saw Allan play for Fulham against Leeds. He noted his ability to control and strike a ball with either foot, his control of a ball with any part of his body and his ability to lay a ball off when tightly marked. Also, his anticipation and sharpness to react first to a half-chance were key reasons to wanting to sign him and ignore people who warned him against it.

After my medical I reported for pre-season training and got to know the other players. I soon found out the gaffer had not quite told me the truth about the wage structure, but that was his way; he wanted to know if I could do it for him. I decided to say nothing and prove myself, then re-negotiate my terms. The first season I set myself a target of twenty goals; I finished top scorer with 26. In my second season I finished top scorer again with 23 goals. I went to see the gaffer because my contract was up. He asked me what I wanted and I asked for a big rise – he just said 'Leave it to me son'. When he said that you knew you had it.

I was delighted to be joining Leeds United. They had some super individual players who were so ambitious it was frightening. You could also sense that nothing came before the team and it was very apparent that no one player was the star. I loved the team spirit in the Leeds dressing room – we shared the same dressing room, we lunched together and we trained together. In fact, we trained very hard. I could not believe how fit I became. The players had a totally different mentality to my previous colleagues: they didn't know the meaning of the word defeat, and the preparation for

Leeds United club handbook, 1969/70.

Pre-season training, July 1969.

a match was so professional. We looked at our opponents' strengths and weaknesses and were kept relaxed. Training routines were never repetitive and everything was done to make us feel special. It created the perfect environment for us to play in.

My debut for Leeds was against Manchester City in the Charity Shield, a match we won 2-1. The supporters gave me a tremendous welcome when I came out that day, and throughout my time at Leeds I had a great rapport with them. As for my League debut against Tottenham, I knew I was at a top club and was determined to make the most of my opportunity. I wanted to prove I could succeed in a team of international players and justify the faith that Don Revie had shown in me. We beat Tottenham 3-1 and I managed to score one of our goals, just beating Pat Jennings to a through ball before nodding it over him. I remember the headlines next day –THE £165,000 GOAL – I'd arrived!

In the League, Leeds began slowly, winning just two of their opening seven fixtures – one of which, a 4-1 win at Nottingham Forest, took them past Burnley's First Division record of thirty matches undefeated. Everton were the early pacesetters and showed their intent to challenge for the title by defeating Leeds at Goodison, ending their unbeaten run in the process.

Following their first defeat, Leeds clicked into gear, recording twelve victories in sixteen matches to blow the title-race wide open. Three victims were thrashed:

'International United'! From left to right: Lorimer (Scotland), Charlton (England), Clarke (England), Jones (England), Gray (Scotland), Madeley (England), Cooper (England), Hunter (England), Giles (Eire), Reaney (England), Sprake (Wales), Bremner (Scotland).

Debut goal for Leeds against Tottenham.

The headline says it all!

Nottingham Forest 6-1, Ipswich 4-0 and West Ham 4-1 – the victory over the Hammers finally pulled back Everton's eight-point advantage. A loss at Newcastle was soon forgotten as Chelsea (5-2) and West Brom (5-1) were put to the sword. With seven league games to go, Leeds were looking good to defend their title, but a fixture crisis was looming because they were also in the FA Cup and European Cup semi-finals…

My first season at Leeds was incredible. It was so different to anything I'd ever experienced. We went for everything and as the season went on we got closer and closer to the treble. In the League we were vying with Everton for the title, and in the FA Cup I remember playing Sutton United in the fourth round: it was like a training session and I scored four in our 6-0 win. Victories over Mansfield and Swindon put us in the semi-finals, where we faced Manchester United. We knew it would be difficult, and it was. It took three games to get through, Billy coming up trumps with a great strike at Burnden Park. They were really tough games, but for me we just had the edge and deservedly reached Wembley.

Our European Cup campaign began against part-timers Lyn Oslo. We demolished them 10-0, and our 16-0 aggregate win is still a club record. In the next round we easily defeated Ferencvaros 6-0 on aggregate before two hard-fought 1-0 wins saw off a very good Standard Liège side. What I recall most about the clash with Liège was arriving at their ground and being refused entry. We got off the coach and started walking in through a side door raging – after that we couldn't wait to start.

Unfortunately, the Liège clashes were the start of serious fixture congestion for Leeds, and this took a toll on the team. By the time Leeds faced Celtic in the semi-final first leg at Elland Road they'd played eight matches since the initial Liege win, including the Manchester United trilogy. In addition, this match was the end of a four-match sequence in seven days. After their initial clash with Manchester United, Geoffrey Green of *The Times* observed. 'They say they (Leeds) relish hard work, that the expense of energy seems an eternal delight. But surely there must be a limit.'

Green was correct: something had to give. Revie rested players for the final six League fixtures. In fact, he had little choice in this as the club doctor had identified five

Allan tries his luck in a League encounter against Wolves.

One of four Allan struck against Sutton in the FA Cup.

Another FA Cup goal … this time against Mansfield.

Scoring against Swindon.

Semi-final action against Manchester United.

Celebration time after Billy's goal books Leeds' trip to Wembley.

Thumbs up from the Leeds players taking a well earned soak after knocking Manchester United out of the Cup at Burnden Park.

We're there!

first-teamers as being mentally and physically fatigued. After a defeat at home to Southampton, Tom German of *The Times* wrote, 'If they (Leeds) lose the championship, it is because of commitments heaped on them by the rewards of their own talents.' The last six games would yield just a single win over Burnley, when Eddie Gray scored his 'goal in a million'. Leeds ended the campaign runners-up and focused their attention solely on the final stages of the cup competitions they were still in … beginning with the semi-final of the European Cup.

Against Celtic there's no doubt we were jaded and went down to a first-minute strike. That said, Jimmy Johnstone was magnificent.

By the time Leeds lined up for the FA Cup final, the players had rested for seven days. They looked rejuvenated but the pitch was in a disgraceful state, due to the Horse of the Year Show taking place on it a few days before the final and heavy rain.

> Chelsea *v*. Leeds United, 1970 FA Cup final.
> *Chelsea*: Bonetti, Webb, McCreadie, Hollins, Dempsey, Harris (captain), Baldwin, Houseman, Osgood, Hutchison, Cooke, Hinton (substitute).
> *Leeds United*: Sprake, Madeley, Cooper, Bremner (captain), Charlton, Hunter, Lorimer, Clarke, Jones, Giles, Gray, Bates (substitute).

Allan on his European Cup debut against Lynn Oslo.

Allan tries in vain to equalise against Celtic.

Leeds United: 1970 FA Cup final squad. From left to right, back row: Reaney, Sprake, Harvey, Cooper. Middle row: Bremner, Hunter, Charlton, Madeley, Yorath. Front row: Gray, Lorimer, Giles, Bates, Clarke, Jones, Hibbitt, Belfitt.

They put sand down, but as the game wore on it was like playing in quicksand. However, Eddie Gray overcame horrendous conditions to give a virtuoso performance and deservedly won the Man of the Match award. We should have won: at times it was just one way-traffic. I know they had their chances, but we should have buried them – we were so much in control. Unfortunately, Gary had a rush of blood with the first goal, and we simply failed to finish the chances we made. It was a great game to play in though.

The 2-2 draw meant a first Cup final replay in fifty-eight years, but the papers were delighted with the game. Geoffrey Green wrote, 'It was not a classic but an epic … the finest final seen at Wembley since the war…it had everything from A to Z.' After Wembley, Leeds' next game was in the European Cup.

We flew to Edinburgh for the return with Celtic. The match was switched to Hampden Park because so many people wanted to see the game. The atmosphere was electric; it was absolutely brilliant. The attendance of 136,000 is still a European gate record. We had a great start when Billy leathered one in from thirty-five yards, but they ended up winning 2-1 on the night to go through on aggregate. Looking back, they were the better team over the two matches, but I'd loved to have played them a couple of years later, when I believe we were at our peak.

Relaxing before the FA Cup final, the Leeds United way!

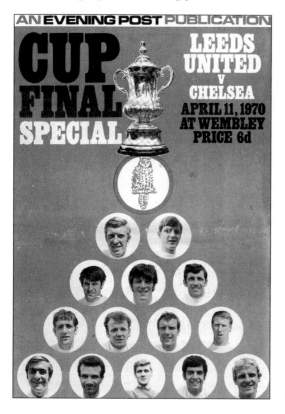

Yorkshire Evening Post *FA Cup final special.*

HRH Princess Anne is introduced to Leeds prior to the kick-off.

Leeds on the attack during their thrilling 2-2 draw with Chelsea.

Allan watches on as his strike partner scores Leeds' second goal at Wembley.

After a season promising so much, only the FA Cup remained. The tired Leeds squad would have two weeks to prepare.

> Chelsea *v*. Leeds United, 1970 FA Cup final replay.
> *Chelsea*: Bonetti, Webb, McCreadie, Hollins, Dempsey, Harris (captain), Baldwin, Houseman, Osgood, Hutchison, Cooke, Hinton (substitute).
> *Leeds United*: Harvey, Madeley, Cooper, Bremner (captain), Charlton, Hunter, Lorimer, Clarke, Jones, Giles, Gray, Bates (substitute).

Leeds were refreshed, but Chelsea had also regrouped and altered their formation, meaning that Ron Harris would be marking Eddie Gray, not David Webb, who'd been given a roasting at Wembley. In a game summed up by Geoffrey Green as 'one with vicious tackling – Boadiccea might have been on parade', Mick Jones gave Leeds a first-half lead but Chelsea proved resilient once again when Osgood equalised near the end. In a cruel twist of fate, Webb exacted his revenge for his Wembley torment with an extra-time winner.

Amazingly, finishing with nothing brought us sympathy from the press for a short while, who were convinced that fatigue and fixture congestion had denied us any success. During the run-in, of course tiredness crept in – you can't play that many matches without it effecting you – but you put it to the back of your mind. You're in the semi-final

Don Revie rallies his troops before extra time in the replay.

of the FA Cup: you don't want to lose; you're second in the League: you want to keep the pressure up; you're then playing in a European Cup semi-final: you want to win that. At the time we simply took each match as it came – I know it's an old cliché, but that's all you could do. The defeat made us even more determined for the next season.

Looking back, of course, the FA should have done more to help the fixture congestion, but I wouldn't have changed a thing to be involved in a season like that: it was fantastic. How many players have ever had a chance of going for the treble? Very few, and we nearly did it. It just wasn't to be.

Some people said we had a bad season ... bad season? The majority of players would go though an entire career without coming close to what we achieved – and that was my first season with the club, I loved it. Admittedly we lost out in everything, and I'm a terrible loser – I hated that and of course I was disappointed we ended the season with no silverware – but to be involved right to the death was fantastic, and we had season after season like that. We were always in for something.

Whenever Leeds supporters talk to me about the 1969/70 campaign they believe it was one of the club's greatest ever and it was. Leeds United was the team to beat and I was playing for them. Life could not have been better.

6

THE GREATEST SHOW ON EARTH

The domestic campaign may have been over, but for Allan Clarke there was no respite as the World Cup finals in Mexico was weeks away.

Since first being involved with the Under-23s in 1966, I had been in every squad Alf picked, but I still had to make my full debut. This disappointed me because I'd scored regularly for my clubs throughout the period and played six times for the Under-23s. I knew I was up against Hurst, Osgood and so on, but after four years I couldn't do any more to impress him. I was also used to being around world stars like Bobby Moore, Alan Ball, Geoff Hurst, Bobby Charlton and Gordon Banks – I'd played against them numerous times and felt a part of the squad, which many of us thought was stronger in depth than it had been in 1966.

Alf was a great man and manager, but before flying out in 1970 I told Margaret if I didn't get a game I'd drop out of the next squad because I really felt I should have been given a chance in the full side. I played in two 'B' internationals during our acclimatisation against Colombia and Universitaria before we moved onto our base in Guadalajara.

After defeating Rumania 1-0 and losing by the same score to Brazil in an unforgettable encounter, Alf came over to me during training the day before our clash with Czechoslovakia and told me I'd be playing. In his next breath he said he thought I was now ready! Though I was delighted, his last comment did annoy me because players had come into a squad for the first time and won a cap immediately. Nevertheless, it was a great moment for me knowing I'd finally be representing my country and it wasn't a meaningless game: we needed to win to qualify for the quarter-finals.

At the team meeting before the match with Czechoslovakia, Alf asked who would take a penalty. I sat there waiting for one of the more experienced players to come forward, but no one did, so I volunteered. Alf said fine. Before a game, Alf never really talked too much about the opposition, it was more about what we did. Just before going out he had a little word with each of us. All he'd say to me was, 'Allan just play as you do for Leeds', simple as that.

England *v*. Czechoslovakia: Banks (Stoke), Newton (Everton), Cooper (Leeds), Mullery (Tottenham), Charlton J. (Leeds), Moore (West Ham, captain), Bell (Manchester City), Charlton R. (Manchester United), Astle

The 'Magnificent Seven'. The seven Leeds players chosen in England's 'provisional' World Cup squad in 1970. From left to right: Cooper, Reaney, Jones, Hunter, Madeley, Clarke, Charlton.

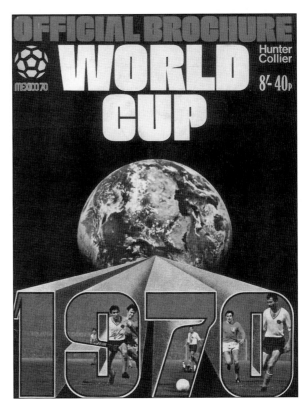

One of many brochures for the 1970 World Cup finals in Mexico.

England's 1970 World Cup squad.

Spot on! Allan scores on his England debut against Czechoslovakia.

Allan shows off his first 'full' England cap.

Allan in the England shirt he wore on his debut against Czechoslovakia in 1970 . . . and with his cap.

(West Brom), Clarke (Leeds), Peters (Tottenham) Substitutes: Osgood (Chelsea), Ball (Everton).

In a game of few chances we finally got a break when Kuna handled for a penalty. I looked around and could sense some of my colleagues wondering if it was wise that I was taking it. However, I was really confident. I put the ball on the spot and sent Viktor the wrong way for what proved to be the winner. In the dressing room afterwards, Les Cocker came over and said, 'Allan, before you slotted the penalty away Alf asked, "Will he score?" and I told him, 'Put your mortgage on it, no danger!' That was a great day for me, and one I'll never forget.

Disappointingly we went out in the quarter-finals to West Germany, when we really should have won, but it was a fantastic experience to have been involved in what is still acknowledged as the best World Cup ever. During the tournament I saw, without doubt, the greatest ever football side, Brazil's World Cup winning team. They had unbelievable players: today Pele, Gerson, Jairzinho, Tostao, Rivelino and Carlos Alberto are instantly recognisable names throughout football. Since 1970, Brazil have produced many world-class players in their own right, like Zico, Socrates, Ronaldo and Roberto Carlos, but none would have got into Brazil's class of '70 – they were out of this world.

I also saw at close quarters the greatest player ever, Pele. In every sport there is one person who stands out as the undisputed 'king'. Pele was, and always will be, the greatest footballer of all time. He had everything; pace, skill, touch, controlled aggression, strength, was great in the air and on the ground, and he scored over a thousand goals. What more can you say, in terms of all-round ability. He had the lot; he was brilliant.

Mind you, we had some world-class stars ourselves. Gordon Banks was the best goalkeeper of his era. Many of his saves are legendary now, especially his classic one from Pele's header in our group match with Brazil in Guadalajara that summer. He was never what some would call flamboyant: he would always just make the simple save rather than look for the spectacular for the sake of it.

In front of him was Bobby Moore, who was a wonderful ambassador for English football. He had style, charisma and the more pressurised an occasion, the better he played. This was never better illustrated than in his performance against Brazil. You never saw him at his best for West Ham, but once he put on that England shirt he was world class. I loved playing with Bobby; he never bawled players out, he was the encouraging type. I first played with him when representing the Football League against the Scottish League and he got me out of trouble several times with the right call. Without doubt, Bobby was the best reader of the game football has produced.

In midfield Alan Ball was a real dynamo and would be running as powerfully in the last minute as the first. Fiery and passionate, his quick temper occasionally got the better of him, but what a wonderful player. Just behind our front two was Bobby Charlton, who like the skipper was a tremendous ambassador for English football. A wonderful player with a terrific shot, I think Bobby retired too early, because in Mexico he was outstanding. Another great all-rounder, he had everything.

The final player I would pick out as outstanding from our side was Martin Peters. Commentators used to say he was 'ahead of his time'. I'm not quite sure about that, but he used to make wonderful late runs which caused havoc for defences. Although he wasn't the fastest player, he was a great team player and scored his share of important goals.

7

TINKLER'S BLUNDER AND EUROPEAN GLORY
1970/71

What a difference twelve months had made to Allan Clarke's life. From the depression of his time at Leicester, he had played in the World Cup and settled into life at Leeds.

At Leeds nothing was routine; everything had a purpose. Before every game, the gaffer insisted we stayed at a hotel to prepare. For home matches we went to the Craiglands in Ilkley, but this changed during the 1970/71 campaign after the gaffer agreed to our request to only stay if we had a major European match. Following our evening meal we would relax by playing carpet bowls or bingo. Many observers laughed at this practice, but we loved it – it was our way of winding down.

On match day we'd have a walk round the hotel before our pre-match meal and team talk, where the gaffer would go through the dossiers on our opponents. Before a match we all had our particular superstitions. I always put my shirt on first, then, slips, shorts, socks and boots; finally I'd get any plasters and tie-ups I needed. Billy and I used to have a couple of caps of whisky before a game. The gaffer would come in about thirty minutes before kick off and join us for one. If we got kicked we never felt it as much! I also liked to go out of the dressing room last. At Leeds, Jack also liked this superstition, so I came out second last until he retired. I've no idea why I did I, it's just something that happened.

As for training, I loved it. Our five-a-side and eight-a-side games were particularly competitive. We'd practice situations from throw-ins, wall passing, all sorts. Then we'd switch to shooting, and that meant everyone. I would also practice one-on-ones, which was a big part of my game.

Generally we never really practised set pieces, which surprised many people because we scored a stack of goals from corners and free kicks. When it came to deep free kicks we had loads of options. We either played it deep to Jack, Jonah or myself, short down the flanks or through the middle. If it was within range of goal, Peter would invariably leather it and all we did was make sure that we had a player in the wall to cause a diversion and another player looking for the follow-up if the 'keeper fumbled.

Probably the best-known tactic built around a single player was for Jack Charlton, particularly at corner kicks. Jack was brilliant in the air and our opponents never really countered his aerial threat, because if the 'keeper or defender got it away there was always another player waiting to pounce. If we won a penalty kick, though I took them for England, I was way down the list for Leeds, Peter and John made sure of that and to be fair they rarely missed.

Defensively, we all had our instructions from the gaffer. Terry covered the left post, Paul Reaney the right. I used to defend the near post and Jonah would pick one of their centre-halves up, as the other generally stayed behind. Jack and Norman would follow the strikers, and Billy and John would mark their opposite number. We were always organised: if any opponent won the ball it rarely ended up where it was intended to go.

Leeds began the season in scintillating fashion, winning their opening five fixtures against Manchester United, Tottenham, Everton, West Ham and Burnley. A further four-game winning sequence in November against Blackpool, Stoke, Wolves and Manchester City helped them to an opening run of twenty-four games with just a single defeat.

The 1-0 victory at Maine Road, where an Allan Clarke strike settled a magnificent match, was summed up by James Wilson of the *Sunday Times* 'There was present…the touch of inspiration, which turns a good team into a great one. Leeds normally field seven or eight brilliant players, and their whole squad does not include a weak performer. Quality and ability are at the root of their consistency.'

Leeds United, 1970/71. From left to right, back row: Galvin, Yorath, Harvey, Jones, Sprake, Charlton, Clarke, Hunter, Gray, Madeley. Front row: Belfitt, Reaney, Lorimer, Giles, Bremner, Cooper, Bates, Hibbitt.

Back with a bang! Allan returns from injury with a goal against Manchester City.

Allan and Margaret entertain Frank before a league fixture with Ipswich.

With eight games remaining, Leeds held a six-point lead, but Arsenal had two games in hand. Leeds followed up a defeat at Chelsea with a 4-0 win over Burnley, Allan scoring all four. Arthur Hopcraft of *The Observer* was impressed, 'He accepts possibilities and alternatives with exceptional speed, and yet has such control that he never looks hurried when he exploits them. Only the frantic behaviour of opposing players around him reveals how sudden and punishing much of his work is.'

Arsenal were, however, still gnawing away at Leeds' points advantage, and the crunch fixture that swung the title their way came on 17 April when Leeds faced West Brom, who were without an away win in sixteen months, at Elland Road. The match was officiated by Ray Tinkler.

At the beginning of the season the gaffer told us 'Forget last season, we've got to start all over again. We've done it before, we can do it again.' We had been at the top of the League all season until we entertained West Brom. We hadn't played that well and just after half time, already a goal down, Jonah had a perfectly good goal disallowed. We started coming forward again and Tony Brown intercepted Norman Hunter's pass and broke across the half-way line. The linesman immediately raised his flag, because Colin Suggett was returning from a previous attack and was clearly offside. The Leeds players and Suggett stopped, but referee Tinkler waved play on. Brown carried the ball forward before squaring it to Astle, who, also offside, side-footed the

They shall not pass! Unfortunately, later in the game West Brom did.

Leeds fans invade the pitch following West Brom's 'offside goal'.

ball into an empty net.

The crowd erupted, fans invaded the pitch, the Leeds players and the gaffer protested. I can still see him looking up at the heavens after the pitch invasion, but the referee was adamant, the goal stood. My late goal was mere consolation. Tinkler required a police escort after the game and never refereed at Elland Road again – and rightly so because his mistake cost us the Championship that season. In the dressing room we went crackers, but what could we do? The destiny of the title was now out of our control. It was the first time the ground had been invaded like that and such a situation was created purely by a referee's diabolical decision.

Match of the Day was beginning to analyse key moments in a game and televised the match that evening. During the commentary after the controversial goal, Barry Davies' comment that 'Leeds are going mad, and they have every right to' summed up everyone's feelings at the time.

You don't see on the film the linesman putting his flag up immediately after Norman's pass was intercepted, but by far the worst part of the incident was when Brown squared the ball across Gary Sprake for Astle to tap in. Astle had to be offside because our only defender, Paul Reaney, was still chasing back and is clearly behind him when he scored. Astle couldn't have been onside.

The decision was scandalous. It was all over the papers, Don even went on TV for a debate, but the score stood. It was, without doubt, the worst refereeing decision ever during my career. We won our remaining games, but Arsenal had games in hand and clinched the title by a point in their last match at Tottenham. The London derby wasn't the key: Tinkler's decision against West Brom had cost us the title and nine months' hard work.

In the FA Cup, Leeds overcame the challenge of Swindon in the fourth round 'With the nonchalance of a traveller depositing a paper towel in its receptacle after a wash and brush up' according to Richard Bott of the *Sunday Express*. Colchester United of the Fourth Division awaited Leeds next.

At the start of my career I was part of a Walsall team that caused a huge shock when we knocked out Stoke City. In '71 I experienced the other side when Leeds lost in the FA Cup to Colchester United. Billy missed the game due to injury and never stopped reminding us for years after! Without taking anything away from what was a tremendous victory for Colchester, at times we did play with injuries and the day before, when we flew to a local seaside resort, I shouldn't have travelled. At the hotel I went straight to bed; I had no strength at all. The gaffer sent for a doctor and I was given an injection, which knocked me out until Saturday morning.

When I woke up I did feel better but my ribs were really painful whenever I breathed in. I went downstairs and saw Rod Belfitt, who was driven down the evening

The biggest upset of them all: Colchester 3 Leeds 2.

Allan scores against Sparta Prague during Leeds march to the Fairs Cup final.

before in case I didn't make it. I wasn't right but when the gaffer wanted you to play you did and we all played through the pain barrier many times. How I got through the match I'm not sure. We lost 3-2, when again Gary dropped the odd clanger. It was one of the greatest cup shocks ever and the media never allowed us to forget it. On the way back I still wasn't felling too good, before the gaffer told me I'd done really well because I had pleurisy. I was stunned, but I still played the following week.

Leeds now had just one chance left to avoid a repeat of the previous season and win some silverware.

We fought our way through the opening rounds of the Fairs Cup competition, defeating Sarpsborg, Dynamo Dresdon, Sparta Prague and Victoria Setubal. Only Liverpool stood in our way of the final. Anfield was always one of my favourite grounds to play at, because Liverpool supporters always gave us a tremendous reception even though they were desperate for their own team to win. We always had close encounters, and our semi-final in the Inter-Cities Fairs Cup was no exception.

As usual the match was tight, and it was left to Billy, who had been out for a long time and played in attack with me because Jonah was injured, to settle the tie with a great header. The second leg was a tense affair because the gaffer was forced to play Joe Jordan as a lone front man after Jonah and myself went off through injury. We packed the midfield and succeeded in smothering Liverpool's attacks, winning through by virtue of Billy's header at Anfield.

The final against Juventus was the last ever, as it was to be replaced by the UEFA

Cup the following season, so we were well aware that a bit of history could be made if we won. They had a fabulous team, which included Bettaga, Anastasi (who had joined them for a world-record transfer fee), Capello and Causio. When we arrived in Turin on the Monday it was belting with rain, and never stopped for three days. During the team talk in Turin I remember the gaffer saying the pitch was waterlogged and had so much surface water on it that the match could turn into a farce. He could not believe it was going ahead, but we had to get on with it.

We went down to the stadium, warmed up and started the match. The rain was torrential. You couldn't judge anything at all – as soon as the ball hit the ground it stopped. After about twenty minutes, Eddie Gray slipped awkwardly and had to go off. At half time we tried to get the game abandoned but the referee refused, although eventually he had no choice but to abandon it shortly after half time.

> Juventus *v.* Leeds United, 1971 Fairs Cup final, first leg.
> *Juventus*: Piloni, Spinosi, Marchetti, Furino, Morino, Salvadore, Haller, Causio, Anastasi, Capello, Bettaga, Novellini (substitute).
> *Leeds United*: Sprake, Reaney, Cooper, Bremner (captain), Charlton, Hunter, Lorimer, Clarke, Jones, Giles, Madeley, Bates (substitute).

Two days later the match was replayed and we played brilliantly to draw 2-2. Juventus took the lead a little against the run of play through Bettaga, before Paul

Both benches shelter from a torrential downpour during the ill-fated Fairs Cup final first leg.

Allan follows up Paul Madeley's equaliser in Leeds' 2-2 draw in Turin.

Yorkshire Evening Post *Fairs Cup final special.*

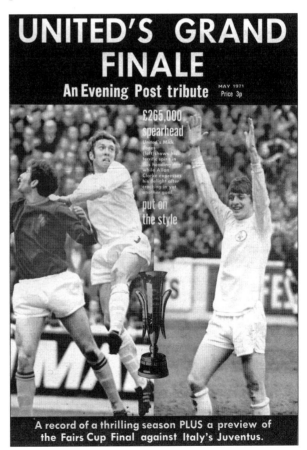

Above and below: First blood from this strike by Allan. Leeds won on the away goals rule.

Madeley's speculative 25-yard drive wrong-footed their goalkeeper. Juventus regained the lead through Capello but near the end Mick Bates, on for Jonah, volleyed home with his first touch.

Leeds United *v*. Juventus, 1971 Fairs Cup final, second leg.
Leeds United: Sprake, Reaney, Cooper, Bremner (captain), Charlton, Hunter, Lorimer, Clarke, Jones, Giles, Madeley, Bates (substitute).
Juventus: Tancredi, Spinosi, Marchetti, Furino, Morino, Salvadore, Haller, Causio, Anastasi, Capello, Bettaga, Novellini (substitute).

The return at Elland Road was a really exciting match. I gave us an early lead, before Anastasi capitalised on a rare defensive mix-up to equalise. There were chances at both ends and the result was in doubt right to the end, but we hung on relatively comfortably to win the trophy by virtue of the away-goals rule. I was obviously pleased for all the lads after the disappointments of the last couple of seasons, but this triumph was extra-special to me because it was my first major honour.

On the international front, I won five caps during the season. I scored in victories over East Germany 3-1 and Malta 5-0, then helped England win the Home International Championship with victories over Scotland 3-1 and Northern Ireland 1-0, a match in which I scored the only goal, and a draw with Wales. I was delighted to have finally broken into the first team on a regular basis and looked forward to more honours.

England's squad before their 1971 Home International clash with Wales. From left to right, back row: Shilton, Smith, Lloyd, Nish, Lawler, Brown, Hughes, McFarland, Clemence, Banks, Moore, Peters, Chivers. Front row: Madeley, Coates, Clarke, Cooper, Hurst, Kidd, Storey, Ball, Lee, Harvey.

8

UP FOR THE CUP
1971/72

During the 1971/72 season Leeds overcame the difficulty of playing their first three 'home' League games on neutral grounds, due to the pitch invasion against West Brom, to play some of the best attacking football ever witnessed at Elland Road. To begin with, however, it was hard work, especially as Clarke and Jones were injured for much of the time. A defeat at Coventry in October resulted in Revie bringing back his first-choice strike pairing earlier than planned. Starting with a 3-0 win over Manchester City, six victories in seven games followed, including a 1-0 win at leaders Manchester United. By Christmas, Leeds were just five points adrift and, after a two-goal victory at Anfield on New Year's Day, they were back in the pack with a fully fit squad.

Between January and March, Leeds put together a run comprising eleven victories, four draws and just a single defeat – but, even more importantly, they played arguably their best football under Don Revie's management. In the League, Leeds destroyed Manchester United 5-1, Southampton 7-0, Arsenal 3-0 and Nottingham Forest 6-1 and advanced into the semi-finals of the FA Cup again. These results, the first two in particular, brought rave reviews. Leeds' sustained possession game made neutrals gasp when watching them on *Match of the Day*'s televised coverage.

Tony Pawson of the *Observer* wrote, 'In a second half of ceaseless excitement, Leeds annihilated Manchester United, reducing their defence to fumbling incompetence.' Brian Glanville of the *Sunday Times* concurred, 'The spectacle was almost that of the matador toying with a weary bull, the delighted roars of the crowd at each new piece of virtuosity the equivalent of the "Oles" of the bullring.'

We roasted Manchester United at Elland Road, scoring all our goals in the second half; Jonah grabbed a hat-trick. I know they had some great players, but during my time at Leeds, Manchester United won no trophies and were definitely on the decline. During the fifteen games I played against them for Leeds, we rarely lost.

Of the slaying of the Saints, Michael Worth of the *Sunday Express* wrote 'Leeds United unveiled a treasure trove of memorable football riches … if it all seemed too easy, it was only because superb Leeds made it look that way … Southampton belonged to another league. Leeds to another world.'

We thrashed Southampton! Any boy who plays or watches football should see a video

Leeds United squad: 1971/72. From left to right, back row: Belfitt, Hunter, Sprake, Harvey, Jordan, Yorath. Middle row: Faulkner, Galvin, Jones, Madeley, Clarke, Charlton. Front row: Reaney, Bates, Lorimer, Giles, Bremner, Davey, Cooper.

Coventry's 'keeper Bill Glazier makes a fine save from Allan. Leeds won 1-0.

Nicely does it! Allan scores a goal against Arsenal in a 3-0 win.

Allan looks on as Mick Jones scores in the 5-1 hammering of Manchester United.

Allan scores one of his two goals in the 7-0 annihilation of Southampton.

of that match, because that is how football should be played. From a manager's point of view, you always wanted your team to perform well, but you knew you would never get perfection. I believe our performance that afternoon was as near perfection from eleven players as you could get. Everything that is good about football you saw that day. There were great goals, tremendous saves, wonderful pieces of individual skill; you name it, it was in that ninety minutes of football.

What summed up our performance was our sixth goal by Jack, because it was made by brilliant left-wing play from Norman Hunter, whose cross Jack headed in at the far post. Our two centre-halves combining to score, that tells anyone how much on top we were.

When we were keeping possession in the last five minutes – we were 7-0 up at the time – commentators said we were taking the mick ... we weren't. Our instructions were to keep out of trouble because we had an important game coming up, and it would have been ridiculous to get a late injury. Of course we played well that day, ask the Leeds players whether the game flew; they'll tell you it did. Ask a Southampton player and they'll tell you it was like an eternity and they wanted the game to end. What a performance though.

On a historical note, this campaign was the only one during Allan's time at Leeds when League doubles were recorded over both Manchester United and Liverpool. In fact it was only the second occasion a League double had been recorded against either side in the club's history. Leeds may have been out of Europe, but they were on the march in the FA Cup and chasing the double...

After losing to Colchester the previous season we were determined to give the FA Cup a real go and swiftly made progress. I missed our 4-1 win in the third round against Bristol Rovers, but was back for our trip to Liverpool. We defended well to earn a replay, which due to an industrial dispute kicked-off at 2.30 p.m.

Brian James of the *Sunday Times* wrote, 'At full throttle from start to finish, they lacked only the precision among their forwards for the crucial thrust. Hunter and Madeley were in such form in Leeds' defence that mere passion would not do.' James sensed the job was already done. He was right.

There was an incredible atmosphere at the ground and when we ran out for the replay it was absolutely packed. There were fans on the roof of the Scratching Shed behind the goal, and others perched on top of the Old Peacock Pub; they were every- where. I had a bit of stick from the press leading up to the match about my overall

There's no way through in this exciting cup battle at Anfield. Leeds won the replay 2-0.

game, so was delighted to grab both our goals. My second in particular gave me a lot of pleasure. It was one of the best I ever scored and it put us through.

A brace of goals from John Giles at Cardiff took Leeds still further for a clash with Tottenham in the quarter-finals. Michael Boon of the *Sunday Express* summed up Leeds' fifth-round triumph as 'Smooth as cream … Leeds are as rich in talent as any club side in the world.' Against Tottenham, Leeds again produced a performance that had the journalists drooling. Brian James of *The Sunday Times* thought the game had 'As many moments of near perfection as football can get', while Eric Todd of the *Guardian* believed that 'On this form Leeds are irresistible.'

We wore stocking tags for the Tottenham clash and went through our training pre-match routine for the first time. After going a goal behind, when Gary made a horrendous error from a forty-yard free kick, which he misjudged and let in, I hooked home an equaliser on half time to set up the second half. We played some wonderful stuff and thoroughly deserved our win, Jack scoring with a great header from a set piece.

The week before our semi-final, Terry Cooper broke his leg, which was a devastating blow. However, Paul Reaney was now fully recovered from breaking a leg himself, so slotted in at right-back with Paul Madeley switching to the left flank. There was also one other change – and it was a shock – because the gaffer finally gave David Harvey his chance to establish himself in the first team. In some ways he may have been too loyal at times, but that was his style, he knew his best team and wanted to stick to it, but he had finally lost patience with Gary and dropped him.

Birmingham were in the Second Division at the time and tried to psyche us out by copying our pre-match routine, but it backfired; it was a shambles. Midway through the first half Peter pinged over a long ball, I nodded it across and Jonah just popped it in. Peter added a second and, without being overconfident, it was over at half time. Jonah added a third in the second half, but the result was never in doubt.

Reaching Wembley is so important to a player, I experienced both a winning and losing dressing room, and the difference is immense. When the referee blows the whistle at the end of a semi-final and you know you're at Wembley, the feeling is fantastic.

As Cup final preparations began, Leeds were heavily involved in the title shake-up along with Derby, Manchester City and Liverpool. Leeds lost a crucial match at Newcastle three days after their semi-final win, but followed that up with victories over West Brom at The Hawthorns and at home to Chelsea. The FA ruled that Leeds' final match, at Wolves, would have to be played forty-eight hours after the final against Arsenal, along with Liverpool, who also had a game to play.

The build-up to the final was as frantic as ever. Apart from organising tickets, we had to record our 'Cup Final' song and be measured for our match-day suit. I am not sure which was more embarrassing. Our record 'Leeds Leeds Leeds' is still sung today, but is better known as 'Marching on Together'.

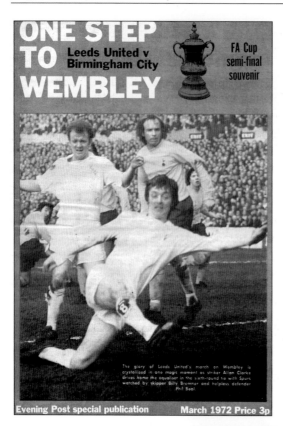

Yorkshire Evening Post *FA Cup semi-final special.*

Celebration time after another goal in the semi-final win over Birmingham.

Popstars! The players record their Cup Final song.

The night before the match we had our usual game of bingo and carpet bowls before watching a video of our win over Southampton. The gaffer's close friend Herbert Warner was also there, cracking jokes as usual: he was great for our morale. Herbert was a lovely man; you could have a lot of fun with him without him ever really taking offence. We were relaxed and ready.

On the morning of the match the gaffer was determined to keep our routine the same. After our pre-match meal we watched a bit of Cup Final Grandstand *before the main team talk. We went through the dossier of the Arsenal players and the game tactics, then set off for Wembley. When the coach turned into Wembley Way it was a fantastic sight, supporters were everywhere.*

> Arsenal *v*. Leeds United, 1972 FA Cup final.
> *Arsenal*: Barnett, Rice, McNab, Storey, McLintock (captain), Simpson, Armstrong, Ball, Radford, Graham, George, Kennedy (substitute).
> *Leeds United*: Harvey, Reaney, Madeley, Bremner (captain), Charlton, Hunter, Lorimer, Clarke, Jones, Giles, Gray, Bates (substitute).

Once at the stadium I felt at home. I loved playing at Wembley. We had a walk on the pitch and I checked both penalty areas for divots and on our way back to the changing rooms the television reporters interviewed us. At about 2.30 p.m. the gaffer gave us his final instructions. As we lined up in the dressing room the gaffer had a

Goal *magazine's FA Cup final special.*

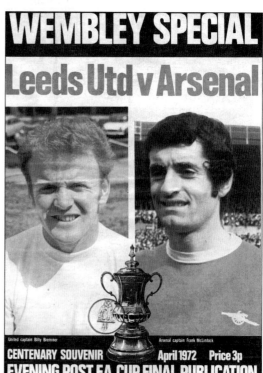

Yorkshire Evening Post *FA Cup final special.*

Match programme for the 1972 FA Cup final.

quick word with each of us; as always he said to me, 'Allan if you're left one-on-one with the goalkeeper just shake your body go past him and put it in the net'. Waiting in the tunnel was tense because we just wanted to get out there. I remember Peter Simpson trying to psyche me out, and I remember thinking, 'This is it ...'

The gaffer led us out of the tunnel into the wall of sound that greeted us. We passed through a special presentation party to commemorate the Centenary Final on our stroll to the halfway line. It was fantastic. The Queen wished us all luck, then we ran to our supporters and the tension drained away.

Arsenal had won the double the year before and their team was full of household names like us. The only possible chink was their goalkeeper, Geoff Barnett, who was in for the injured Bob Wilson. In the first half Arsenal had their chances, David Harvey made an excellent reflex save from Frank McLintock and Paul Reaney cleared an Alan Ball volley off the line. We also had our chances. Peter Lorimer had a couple of great attempts and I deflected one of his cross-cum-shots onto the bar just before the interval. At half time the gaffer told us to just carry on as we were because we were the better side and he felt the goal would come.

Eight minutes into the second half we scored, and it's a moment I'll never forget. A ball was played towards me near the half-way line, McLintock was marking me. As I attempted to get away he pushed me. I tried to stay on my feet but actually fell over, then Frank trod on my fingers – it didn't half hurt. Alan Ball got the ball and played it forward; Jack intercepted it. We were now on the attack again. Jack gave the ball to Paul Madeley who played a simple pass forward to Peter Lorimer. I then remember Bill passing me to join the attack. Peter played it to Jonah down the right flank, and I thought, 'I've got to get into the box'. As Jonah took on Bob McNab, I was on the edge of the box. He worked marvels and crossed the ball. As it was coming towards me, I

The teams come out before the Centenary Cup Final in 1972.

Allan heads home the most famous goal in Leeds United's history.

thought 'volley, right-foot volley' and I fancied it. Then, all of a sudden, the ball started to dip, and I realised it wasn't going to reach me, so I thought 'dive'. You only have a second to make your mind up, so I just took off and headed it. I knew it was going in, and obviously it fitted in the corner just nicely.

Over the years I've lost count of how many people have asked me about the goal and introduced me to their children – who weren't even born in 1972. It means so much to so many Leeds United supporters, and it's a very special memory in my football career. Even now when we play Arsenal at Elland Road, supporters sing 'Who put the ball in the Arsenal net, Allan Allan, Who put the ball in the Arsenal net, Allan Allan Clarke' – and that's a wonderful feeling.

After I scored, Charlie George hit the bar, but I always felt we were in control. Peter, Jonah and Eddie Gray all went close, and really we should have won more comprehensively. At the final whistle we hugged one another, then all of a sudden I calmed down and noticed Jonah still lying in Arsenal's penalty area. Les Cocker and Doc Adams were attending to him. I remember Jonah going down but didn't realise the extent of the injury. I went over, but there was nothing we could do; we had to let the medical staff attend to him.

I was told to join the lads, who were lining up to get our medals. Walking up to get our medals was marvellous. I remember kissing it. Also, seeing Billy receive the FA Cup from the Queen and show it to our fans is something I'll never forget: it meant so much to him. Then Jonah went up – I was going to take him, but Norman jumped in ahead of me. I was voted Man of the Match and presented with the trophy after I walked down the steps. The lap of

Billy Bremner raises the FA Cup after Leeds' historic win.

Allan with his 'Man of the Match' award and the lid of the FA Cup!

honour itself was fantastic; it was one of those days when you didn't want to go into the dressing room, you just wanted to stay out on the pitch.

Back in the changing rooms the FA Cup had been filled with champagne and we all drank from it in the bath. We sat in the water for ages just singing. The only sad sight was Jonah, who was resting on a bench in the corner before going to hospital. I sat with him for a while. Within an hour of the final whistle the gaffer said, 'Right lads let's get moving, we're going straight on to the hotel because we have a big match on

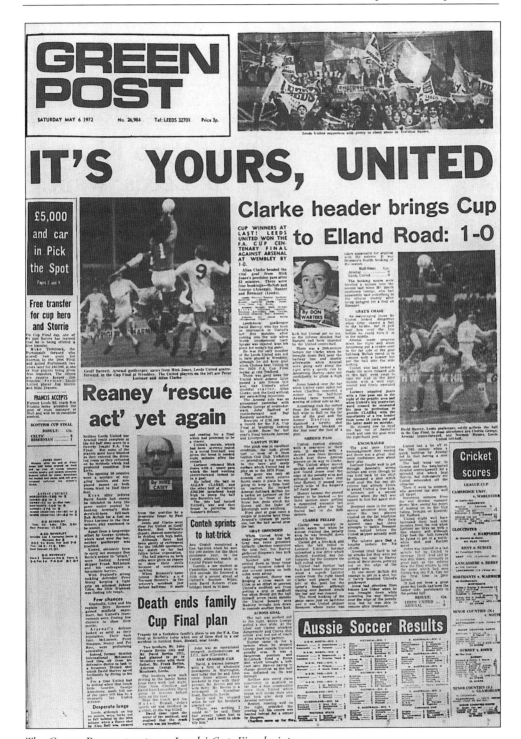

The Green Post *reports on Leeds' Cup Final victory*

Monday night'. We never went to the official banquet, but our wives did. We went to the team coach and drove straight from Wembley with the FA Cup to the Mount Hotel near Wolverhampton. We had dinner at the hotel and Derek Dougan, who lived locally, presented me with the Golden Boot for scoring the winning goal. We all watched Match of the Day *and were interviewed by the BBC.*

They say that you have to experience losing to appreciate the joy of winning. Well, having played in two losing finals before that time, I can honestly say that winning is a whole lot better. Wembley is not a place for losers!

There was also no question that the best team on the day had won the FA Cup. Hugh McIlvanney, of *The Observer* wrote, 'Don Revie's Leeds United, the team who had come to regard Wembley as a place of near misses, won the FA Cup at their third attempt yesterday, when they outplayed Arsenal to an extent that was inadequately reflected in the scoreline. It was Leeds whose football was more controlled, whose ideas the more inventive. Once Leeds had settled, and especially after their goal, they dominated Arsenal confidently.' Frank McGhee, the *Sunday Mirror* correspondent commented, 'Arsenal could have tried for another 100 years and still would not have a serious chance of beating Leeds. Not on the form, the mood and the manpower seen in this Centenary Cup final.' Alan Hoby of the *Sunday Express* recorded that 'The elegant stylists of Leeds have won the FA Cup for the first time. Whatever happens, the beaten finalists of 1965

'*We've won it!*'

and 1970 have at last killed the sneer that they always stumble at the final hurdle. That taunt lies buried forever beneath the damp green turf of Wembley.' David Miller writing for the *Sunday Telegraph* said that 'Leeds, the most consistent team in European soccer for the last eight years, carried off the centenary FA Cup in a final which was eventually one-sided. From the start, Leeds were transparently the better side and by the finish they had outplayed the opposition in almost every phase of the game, even if they only controlled it for that last half-hour.'

Albert Barham, of *The Guardian*, noted that, 'A new name, Leeds United, will be inscribed on the plinth of the FA Cup this centenary year and few will deny that the honour has been long overdue. A spectacularly headed goal by Clarke was insufficient reward for the superiority of Leeds in every department of the game. They could and should have had a couple more afterwards.' Meanwhile, Frank Butler, writing for the *News of the World*, was of the opinion that 'Leeds well deserved their victory after they got out of the Yale-lock grip of the Arsenal defensive system in the first half. A goal was needed to break the Arsenal system and what a great goal Leeds scored. Clarke took it perfectly with his head and Barnett was nowhere near when the ball crossed the line. Leeds had always looked the more classy footballing side. Once they scored they blossomed out like supermen. Suddenly Arsenal looked tired, beaten and very ordinary. Closer to home, Terry Brindle of *The Yorkshire Post* was equally fulsome in his praise 'It was the day on which Leeds United proved beyond question that they are a great side. A day on which the most coveted trophy in soccer was added to their impressive pedigree, and no side which has not won the cup can claim to true greatness.'

However, forty-eight hours later Leeds put in 'one of the bravest footballing failures of all time' according to Eric Todd of *The Guardian,* as they lost 2-1 to Wolves – missing out on valuable points and the double.

There's no doubt in my mind that the FA's insistence the game took place so close to the Cup final affected us. In the dressing room afterwards you'd have thought you were at a funeral. In many ways '72 was far worse than '70 because we'd won the cup and really thought we'd do the double. In hindsight, the aftermath of the pitch invasion against West Brom really caught up with us. If we had played all our games at Elland Road the title would have been wrapped up before the 1972 Cup Final. However, no one could take away the feeling we had immediately after winning the FA Cup that season, it was unbelievable.

After losing out on the double, the team returned to a heroes' welcome at Elland Road with the FA Cup.

Leeds United 1972 FA Cup winners. From left to right, back row: Reaney, Charlton, Harvey, Jones, Hunter, Madeley. Front row: Lorimer, Clarke, Bremner, Giles, Bates, Gray.

9

MIRACLE 'KEEPERS
1972/73

In the League, Leeds got off to a shaky start, winning just five of their opening eleven games. A number of reporters began to write the team off as a 'spent force'. Following a 2-1 defeat at home to Liverpool, Eric Todd of the *Guardian* wrote, 'I think they must accept that Giles and Charlton are past their peak, and that Bremner's overworked batteries are running low … Leeds have achieved many things but now…the writing is on the wall.' Allan and the team were philosophical in the face of such criticism and let their performances on the pitch silence those who doubted the side's ability.

Pundits began to write us off but we responded with a scintillating display and thrashed the defending champions, Derby County, 5-0.

It was the start of a sixteen-match run that included six victories at the turn of the year against West Ham, Birmingham, Newcastle, Tottenham, Norwich and Stoke to put Leeds in among the pacemakers again. Unfortunately, there were echoes of 1970 as Leeds made progress in the FA Cup and European Cup Winners' Cup.

Our FA Cup run began against Norwich City, who took us to three games before we eventually knocked them out 5-0 at Villa Park. I had an injection in a foot injury shortly before the final game. I knew I'd be unable to finish the match but managed a first-half hat-trick before coming off in the second.

After defeating Plymouth and West Brom at Elland Road, we faced a really tough quarter-final tie at Derby County. I enjoyed playing at the Baseball Ground: the atmosphere was always good because the fans were so close to the pitch, although the surface itself was diabolical due to poor drainage. They used to put sand down to help, but it made passing very difficult. We knew it would be tight, and it was. Fortunately, Peter did the business for us near the end with a thunderbolt.

The semi-final against Wolves was played at Maine Road. We were really determined to win after being denied the double the season before by them. As the game wore on, a replay looked the likely outcome until Billy popped up to smash home the winner – it's incredible how many semi-finals he won for us down the years.

In the Cup Winners' Cup, Leeds overcame the hostile atmosphere of Ankara and were more than happy to leave Turkey with a draw. In the return leg, a Jones header proved

Allan scores his first goal of the season against West Brom.

Allan on the attack against Everton.

One of a brace of goals against West Brom in an FA Cup fourth round clash.

Delight on drawing Wolves in the semi-finals.

Leeds attack during the semi-final.

Wembley here we come again!

This strike was enough to take Leeds to the European Cup Winners' Cup final.

sufficient. They faced another awful journey in the next round, to East German side Carl Zeiss Jena and again were happy to leave with a draw. Two goals at Elland Road were more than enough to see them home. By far the easiest tie was the quarter-final match with Rapid Bucharest. Leeds won 5-0 at home, making the return leg a formality.

The semi-final paired us with Hajduk Split and was anything but easy. In the first leg we knew we had to get a lead for the return, because they were formidable at home and we needed something to defend. I knocked a goal in during the second half then got sent off for retaliation. My marker had been kicking hell out of me all night and a few minutes after my goal he crashed into me again and took my legs away; I had a rush of blood and kicked him where it hurts. When I got back into the dressing room, I knew I'd let my team-mates and myself down. In Split, we won through on aggregate after drawing 0-0, but suffered another blow as a booking for Billy meant he would join me watching the final.

In the League, the team had stayed involved till the beginning of April, but following the semi-final victory over Wolves, Leeds won just one of their next five matches to finish third. Don Revie rang the changes in preparation for the Cup final against Sunderland.

Sunderland *v*. Leeds United, 1973 FA Cup final.
Sunderland: Montgomery, Malone, Guthrie, Horswill, Watson, Pitt, Kerr (captain), Hughes, Halom, Porterfield, Tueart, Young (substitute).
Leeds United: Harvey, Reaney, Cherry, Bremner (captain), Madeley, Hunter, Lorimer,

Allan is escorted from the field following his dismissal against Hajduk Split.

1973 FA Cup final squad. From left to right, back row: Cherry, Madeley, Jones, Ellam, Jordan, Charlton. Middle row: Reaney, Galvin, Harvey, Sprake, Hunter, Clarke. Front row: Lorimer, Giles, Bremner, Bates, Gray, Yorath.

Clarke, Jones, Giles, Gray, Yorath (substitute).

In the final against Sunderland we were hot-favourites. Porterfield scored during the first half and they defended very well. The key moment was Montgomery's double save from Trevor Cherry's header and Peter's point blank shot. Both were outstanding and you have to give him credit. Having said that, if Peter had scored I'm convinced we'd have gone on and won, but it wasn't to be.

After our defeat we were accused of underestimating them, but that wasn't true. During their run they knocked out Manchester City and Arsenal, so we knew it would be a hard game. What went wrong? We had lots of possession, numerous chances and far better players, but we failed to score, simple as that. Looking back my main memory is the journey after the game to our hotel for our banquet in the evening. I've never seen so many fans crying after a defeat – it was so obvious they felt we'd let them down, and that hurt more than not winning the cup.

Eleven days after their Cup final defeat, Leeds travelled to Salonika to face AC Milan. The players were unsettled by a newspaper story the day before the game saying that Don Revie was to quit and join Everton. The move never materialised. The final itself was marred due to a scandalous performance by the referee. Some of the decisions Christos Michas made were unbelievable: his bias towards the Italians was outrageous.

The formalities are nearly over as Allan meets the guest of honour.

Montgomery's amazing save wins the cup for Sunderland.

The Greek fans booed Milan after their 1-0 win at the presentation and cheered Leeds. Michas was later suspended over bribery allegations, and never officiated in a professional match again.

The refereeing against AC Milan was diabolical. We never stood a chance. The match should have been replayed at the very least.

The season was also notable because Allan was given an extended run in the full England side.

I hadn't played for England since May 1971 for one reason or another. In 1972/73, however, I was back in the side to play at Hampden Park when the Scottish FA celebrated their centenary. It was a big match for me because the crunch World Cup qualifying games against Poland were coming up and I was desperate to be involved. Also, because so many Leeds players were involved on both sides, it was essential we didn't lose.

Scotland *v.* England: Shilton (Leicester), Storey (Arsenal), Hughes (Liverpool), Bell (Manchester City), Madeley (Leeds), Moore (West Ham, captain), Ball (Arsenal), Channon (Southampton), Chivers (Tottenham), Clarke (Leeds), Peters (Tottenham).

Alf hated the Jocks, and all he said before the game was 'You know who we're playing today, get them beat; if you don't we'll not live it down till next season'. The atmosphere was always electric and you could sense the hatred their fans had for us on the terraces – it was unbelievable. It turned out to be one of my most satisfying games for England, because I scored twice in our 5-0 win. Afterwards I flew back with Billy, Norman, Peter and

Allan receives an Evening Standard *award from Sir Alf Ramsey.*

Taking a breather with Alan Ball after defeating Scotland in May 1973

Paul Madeley – although Billy and Peter were pretty quiet on the journey home!

Allan stayed in the team for the rest of the season and played in six further matches, four of them in the post-season tour. The most crucial game was England's 2-0 World Cup defeat to Poland in Chorzow, where both goals appeared to be offside. The defeat meant England had to win the return to qualify for the finals in West Germany. In the other games of the tour, England drew with Czechoslovakia 1-1, defeated the USSR 2-1 and lost to Italy 2-0.

Goal *magazine's World Cup special for the first of England's matches with Poland.*

England duty with Paul Madeley, Norman Hunter and Les Cocker.

England squad for the 1973 Home Internationals and post-season tour. From left to right, back row: Hunter, Blockley, Summerbee, Clarke, Hughes, Clemence, Parkes, Shilton, Bell, McFarland, Moore, Chivers, Peters, Shepardson (trainer). Front row: Madeley, Macdonald, Storey, Ball, Channon, Richards, Nish, Keegan, Currie.

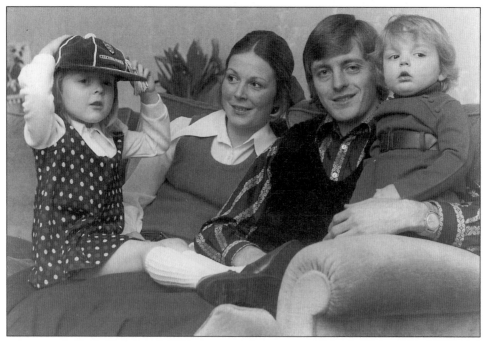

At home in Collingham with Margaret, Sarah and James.

10

CHAMPIONS
1973/74

After the cup heartbreak of the previous season, Leeds began the 1973/74 campaign with a lot to prove.

Pre-season, large sections of the media wrote off our chances of being serious title contenders again. As far as they were concerned we were past it! The gaffer was determined to prove them wrong.

At the team talk before our opening match of 1973/74, the gaffer said, 'Right lads, we've been the best team for the last decade. I know we haven't won as much as we should of, but that's in the past. Now, I've had a thought during the close season, I'd like to know – can we go through the whole season unbeaten.' We all looked at each other in silence and then, after a short while, we said … 'Yes, it's possible'. It was certainly a different pep talk to most seasons. Of course you start off aiming to win all your games, but to actually set it as a target – that was different.

Leeds won their opening seven games against Everton (3-1), Arsenal (2-1), Tottenham (3-0), Wolves (4-1), Birmingham (3-0), Wolves (2-0) and Southampton (2-1). The critics were well and truly put in their place.

Following the seventh win, John Arlott of the *Guardian* wrote 'It was all so controlled, almost amiable … so free from the aura of violence they used to generate.' The winning run ended with a draw against Manchester United, before preparations started for England's build-up for the Poland return with a friendly against Austria at Wembley.

England *v.* Austria: Shilton (Leicester), Madeley (Leeds), Hughes (Liverpool), Bell (Manchester City), McFarland (Derby), Hunter (Leeds), Currie (Sheffield United), Channon (Southampton), Chivers (Tottenham), Clarke (Leeds), Peters (Tottenham, captain).

We annihilated them 7-0. Mick Channon and I both scored two that night, Martin Chivers, Tony Currie and Colin Bell notching the others. My second was particularly memorable. Currie crossed a great ball in to me; I took the weight off it with my chest before selling their right-back a dummy. I then cut into the penalty area before hammering a shot into the far side of the net. I was really pleased, but I should have

Leeds United, 1973/74. From left to right, back row: Lorimer, Gray E., Bates, Clarke, Hunter, McQueen, Ellam, Reaney, Gray, F. Front row: Yorath, Sprake, Cherry, Jordan, Giles, Harvey, Madeley, Bremner, Jones.

What's the problem, Mr Fitzpatrick?

had a hat-trick because Peters was credited with a goal at the end, which I definitely diverted past their goalkeeper. The result was the perfect preparation for our clash with Poland.

After three more games undefeated in the League, Allan reported for the World Cup clash with Poland – the last qualification match for the 1974 World Cup finals. The game turned into one of the most frustrating and disappointing nights in English football history.

Alf picked the same team that lined up against Austria. Our 1-1 draw was classed as a disaster for English football, but that was unfair because we played brilliantly on the night. For me the sickening thing about the game is we only needed to win and we'd qualify, and we felt that as a squad we could have gone a long way in the finals. We had some fantastic players and we were really gelling as a unit. We murdered them on the night, yet somehow only drew.

All the pundits and journalists blamed Norman for the Polish goal, because of his mistimed tackle. I've never agreed with this viewpoint, because Norman was near the halfway line, so there was a long way for their attackers to go. Also, Peter Shilton must have been disappointed with his attempt to save the shot.

The goal apart, nobody could fault our performance. We made chance after chance, only to be thwarted by Tomaszewski, who pulled off some unbelievable saves. He just had one of those nights – one save in particular from me I'll never forget. Near the end a ball came towards me and I volleyed it. As a striker you know when a ball is going in and this was. I raised my arm in triumph and began turning away. I was thinking 'That's it … we've done it!' There was no way he could see the ball because of the bodies in front of him, then suddenly his arm popped out and he's cleared it. I couldn't believe it. At that moment I thought our luck's not in.

The Poland match was the most one-sided international I ever played in – and that includes the 5-0 win over Scotland and 7-0 win over Austria! We paralysed them that night. We were inconsolable in the dressing room after. Alf tried to put a brave face on the situation, telling us we could not have done any more and thanked us for that, but it was impossible to lift us. I was due to make a television commercial the next day for NatWest Bank. The crew came round to my home, but I couldn't do it; I was so disappointed.

It took me weeks to get the game out of my system. I was a first-choice striker and knew the finals were my last opportunity to test myself against the world's best. The only consolation was that we could not have done any more than we did that night. We just never got the break we deserved. Not long afterwards, the FA sacked Alf, which was a disgrace. In hindsight they should have cancelled the previous weekend's fixtures to help us prepare – after all it was the biggest game since the World Cup quarter-final in Mexico. Nowadays, this would never happen, which is absolutely right.

Allan returned to League action the following Saturday. Leeds won their next three games before turning the screw in December with successive victories over Ipswich

Allan in action against QPR.

Penalty, ref! Leeds v. Leicester.

(3-0), Chelsea (2-1), Norwich (1-0) and Newcastle (1-0). They had now gone 22 games undefeated.

We were playing with tremendous confidence and, following convincing victories over Arsenal and Manchester United, our run stood at twenty-nine matches without defeat. Then we lost at Stoke 3-2 after being two-up. Although we were disappointed, we had created an amazing club record that still stands.

By now we only had the Championship to aim for because we were out of all the cups, which was fine by us. Before our next game the gaffer threatened to get the chequebook out if we didn't respond properly to this defeat. This staggered us, because we'd only lost the one game and still had a big points lead over our only rivals Liverpool.

Suddenly, Leeds appeared fallible. Following two draws and a scratchy one-goal win over Manchester City, three successive defeats against Liverpool, Burnley and West Ham sent shock waves around the country.

After their 4-1 defeat at home to Burnley, Brian James in *The Sunday Times* wrote 'Leeds were haunted by doubt, undermined by misunderstandings … their morale … even their reputation was on the verge of destruction'. With just six games remaining,

Allan tries to break the deadlock against Sheffield United during the title run in.

Liverpool could still overhaul Leeds' points total – were Leeds going to blow it again?

The gaffer's comments certainly affected us, because we went through a terrible spell. However, it was during this period that our team spirit came through. Nobody blamed each other, the more experienced players kept encouraging the younger ones to believe in themselves because we knew our form would return, it was just a matter of time.

Sure enough, Leeds had a crucial 2-0 win over Derby, as Liverpool lost to Sheffield United. Both clubs drew their next two fixtures. Leeds went to Sheffield United under immense pressure to win. It became unbearable at half time as news circulated that Liverpool were 4-0 up against Manchester City. Leeds needed inspiration and Peter Lorimer provided it with two priceless goals. That night, the Leeds supporters travelled back up the motorway convinced the title was theirs.

Our final home game of the season was against Ipswich and we knew a win would all but seal the Championship. It was a nerve-wracking encounter, but we should have sewn it up sooner than we did because we took a two-goal lead, before letting them pull back to 2-2 by the hour mark. I remember the groans around the ground when the second went in, but we were not going to let this game slip and I managed to snap up a late chance, which proved to be the winner. The win put us five points clear with a game to go, but Liverpool still had two games in hand.

Ken Jones of the *Sunday Mirror* described the encounter as 'Not so much a game, more an emotional explosion', while Barry Foster of the *Yorkshire Post* summed up everyone's feelings: 'Almost there. That is how Leeds United must feel this morning... the odds on Leeds taking their second League title swung very heavily towards Elland Road.'

In a midweek game, Liverpool had to beat Arsenal to take the title race into the last day of the season. They cracked under the pressure and lost 1-0 to hand us the title. I was at Jonah's house that evening when we heard the result; naturally we were ecstatic. Our final game at QPR was an exhibition match. I managed to score the only goal to close up a wonderful season. We may not have gone the entire season unbeaten, but we dominated throughout. For me, finally winning a Championship medal after being a runner-up on three occasions was the ultimate experience. We'd proved we were the best over a season at last.

Leeds United's record in the League that season was impressive: played 42, won 24, drawn 14, lost 4; goals for 66, goals against 31; 62 points.

Player appearances during the season (with substitute appearances in brackets) were as follows: Harvey 39, Reaney 36, Cherry 37(1), Bremner 42, McQueen 36, Hunter 42, Lorimer 37, Clarke 34, Jones 28(3), Giles 17, Madeley 39, Jordan 25(8), Yorath 23(5), Gray E. 8, Bates 9(1), Gray F. 3(3), Ellam 3(1), Cooper 1(1), Stewart 3, Liddell (1).

Match programme, Leeds v. Ipswich.

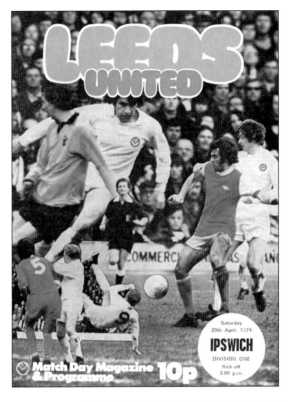

This crucial strike defeated Ipswich and ultimately clinched the First Division title.

Champions!

Leeds United: First Division championship-winning squad. From left to right, back row: Harvey, Jordan, Gray E., Hunter, McQueen, Clarke, Madeley, Reaney, Stewart. Front row: Gray F., Lorimer, Giles, Bremner, Cooper, Bates, Cherry, Yorath.

The goals were scored by: Jones 14, Clarke 13, Lorimer 12, Bremner 10, Jordan 7, Madeley 2, Giles 2, Yorath 2, Bates 2, Cherry 1, own goal 1.

The campaign proved to be the gaffer's last at the club, and what a way to end. Over the years I'd grown very close to him – he was so dedicated to his players and there was nothing he wouldn't do for our families and us. We all shared his ambitions and he trusted us: after a game we'd have a drink, but not excessively, in return he knew we would never let him down. When criticism was required he never shirked the issue, and when the players had disagreements they always stayed within the dressing room. I'd played under him for five seasons and all my major honours came during this period.

The great side was beginning to break up. Trevor Cherry had replaced Terry Cooper at left-back, Gordon McQueen had made the transition in his first season as Jack's replacement and Joe Jordan began to partner myself in attack. In fact, Jonah never regained full fitness after this campaign and retired eighteen months later. Also, Eddie Gray and John Giles were playing less frequently, meaning opportunities for Terry Yorath and Frank Gray.

I've always believed that this was one of the major reasons why Don took the England job during the close season. He would have found it very difficult to drop players he'd brought on since they were kids, but I was still very disappointed. An era was over, and we knew it.

11

EUROPEAN HEARTACHE
1974/75

Post season there was only one story ... who would replace Don Revie at Leeds United ...

There was a lot of speculation. When the Board finally announced Brian would be taking charge, it was a surprise because he had been so outspoken and critical of our tactics as players over the years. A number of us were not happy. Nevertheless, when I reported back for pre-season training along with the other lads, we were a bit surprised to find that Brian was still on holiday: we thought he may want to meet us immediately.

When Brian arrived he looked very nervous. At a team meeting in the players' lounge he obviously wanted to stamp his authority on us, but went completely the wrong way about it. He decided to tell us all exactly what he thought of us – the majority of it was negative – and it was obvious he had no idea how close we were to each other. When he offended one of us he offended us all. When he got to Eddie Gray, he told him that with his injury record, if he was a racehorse he'd have been shot. Those words killed Brian Clough's chances of succeeding at Leeds United. There was deathly silence and no reaction whatsoever. Maybe he said it as a joke, but he'd lost the players' respect and support.

Clough led out Leeds for the first-ever Charity Shield to be played at Wembley, which Liverpool won on a penalty shootout after the match had been drawn in normal time. However, the game was best remembered for Billy Bremner and Kevin Keegan being sent off for no more than a scuffle.

Morale was really low in the squad and it showed on the pitch, Leeds winning just one of their opening seven matches. The Board had to act and they did: Brian Clough was sacked after forty-four turbulent days at Elland Road.

After he left, our form picked up. Jimmy Armfield was installed as manager and – credit to him in difficult circumstances – he stabilised the club. Don Howe arrived as coach, and although Jimmy was a soft touch at times he respected us as experienced footballers and we respected him.

Unfortunately, the damage to the League campaign was done and the players knew

Another season and Allan scores the winner against Birmingham.

A familiar pose: Leeds' number eight wheels away after another goal, this time against Luton.

133

Allan scores one of Leeds' five goals as Sheffield United are put to the sword.

there was no way they could defend their title. However, they soon climbed away from the bottom of the table and produced some fine results, including a 5-1 win over Sheffield United and a 2-1 win at Arsenal, Allan scoring in both games, to eventually finish ninth.

In the FA Cup, Leeds reached the quarter-finals before going out to Ipswich Town after a titanic battle, which went to four games. Earlier in the run, Southern League giant-killers Wimbledon had taken the League champions to a replay. The first game at Elland Road, which ended 0-0, was best remembered for Dickie Guy's late penalty save from Peter Lorimer. Eventually though, the Wombles were eliminated, but they had introduced themselves to football supporters.

With any chance of domestic honours all but gone, attention turned to the big one, the European Cup, which became the target for the season.

We played well in the early rounds and comfortably made the quarter-finals, where we drew Anderlecht. They had some great players in their team, including François Van der Elst, Paul Van Himst and Robbie Rensenbrink. The match was only just completed. In fact we were taken off at one stage because the fog descended so much you couldn't see both goals. We were a goal up at the time through Joe Jordan and wanted desperately to carry on. Fortunately, the fog lifted just enough for us to complete a 3-0 win, but a stronger referee may not have let the match carry on. You

The Wombles invade Elland Road for an FA Cup clash, and leave with a draw!

Action from Leeds' titanic battle with Ipswich in the FA Cup.

Gently does it!

could see he didn't know what to do. In Belgium, the weather was appalling and the pitch was pure mud. We won 1-0, Billy chipping in a great one for us – their 'keeper was so impressed he went up to him following the goal to shake his hand – but the state of us at the end was unbelievable.

Before the draw was made, we really wanted to avoid Barcelona and be away first, but we got Barcelona at home. We knew we were in for one heck of a battle. They were a great side, with some world-class players. Many would have got into any team, the most notable being Johann Cruyff, who at the time was probably the best player in the world.

Billy got us off to a flying start with a great strike and it settled us. We matched them throughout, and although they scored from a free kick in the second half I managed to snap up a chance a few minutes from time to edge us ahead in the tie. Of course we were pleased, but Barcelona were happier because of their away goal.

In Barcelona we had to score first, and Peter did the business for us after about fifteen minutes. We were in control. From there on in it was backs- to-the-wall stuff, as they threw everything at us. Near the end, Gordon McQueen had a rush of blood and got sent off, which made life very difficult – especially when they scored a late goal. Our goalkeeper that night, David Stewart, was magnificent, however, pulling off some unbelievable saves, and we held on for a brilliant result.

Looking back this is my most memorable game in Europe for Leeds. Getting to a European Cup final had been the ultimate ambition for so many people at the club and it meant everything to us. I'll never forget the delight on the players' faces in the dressing room afterwards.

Bayern Munich *v.* Leeds United, 1975 European Cup final.
Bayern Munich: Maier, Durnberger, Andersson, Schwarzenbach, Beckenbauer (captain), Roth, Tortensson, Zobel, Muller, Hoeness, Kapellman. Substitutes: Weiss, Wunder. *Leeds United*: Stewart, Reaney, Gray F., Bremner (captain), Madeley, Hunter, Lorimer, Clarke, Jordan, Giles, Yorath. Substitute: Gray E. (for Yorath).

When we went out to warm up before the final with Bayern Munich we knew it would be hard. They had a number of world stars in their side: Sepp Maier, Franz Beckenbauer and Gerd Muller. However, so did we, so we were not overawed.

Although they were favourites we dominated the first half and the least we deserved was a penalty when Beckenbauer brought me down just before half time. I picked the ball up and went on a run; Beckenbauer came over, I dropped my shoulder and went past him and was about to bend the ball round Maier when he wrapped his legs around me and pulled me down. It was a blatant penalty. When I got to my feet I couldn't believe the referee had given a goal kick. We all appealed, but the referee, who was less than ten yards away from the incident, didn't want to know.

In the second half, Maier made a great stop from Billy before Peter had a tremendous volley harshly disallowed, when Billy was adjudged to have strayed offside. This latter incident was particularly galling, as the referee had initially awarded a goal. We never recovered from this blow and Bayern scored two breakaway goals.

Allan in action against Barcelona at Elland Road.

This strike against Barcelona in the first leg is one of the most crucial goals Allan scored for Leeds.

All smiles as Peter Lorimer scores the opener in the Nou Camp.

It doesn't get bigger than this – the 1975 European Cup final.

The turning point of the final, as Peter Lorimer's thunderbolt is harshly ruled out.

The end of an era. The players thank supporters at a civic reception.

I know we lost but we were by far the better side and deserved our place among the game's elite. We received a great homecoming outside Leeds Civic Hall, but we knew this team's dominance had come to an end. I loved the challenge of playing against the best teams and players throughout Europe. Some of my opponents were incredibly cynical, but that was their style of play and I had to adapt. Yet for all the bad ones, you would also play against individuals with exceptional skill and that's why European football was so special: it was so different to the domestic game. When I was at Walsall I could only dream of such nights, so to be competing regularly against players of this quality was unbelievable. When I look back at my six campaigns in Europe for Leeds, we reached three finals and a semi-final, which was some record.

12
END OF AN ERA
1975-1978

There is no question that Jimmy Armfield inherited the hardest task of any Leeds manager. He knew that he would have to replace legends like Billy Bremner, John Giles and Norman Hunter, whilst at the same time satisfy the expectations of fans who were used to success. That he set about it methodically, and created an attractive and organised side, said much for his managerial ability. As Revie's legends moved on, new faces came into the side. Tony Currie replaced John Giles in midfield, Frank Gray established himself at left-back, with Trevor Cherry moving into midfield. The ever-reliable Paul Madeley partnered Gordon McQueen in defence. Allan Clarke still led the attack in tandem with Joe Jordan, with Carl Harris and Arthur Graham supporting on the flanks.

Leeds finished the 1975/76 season in a creditable fifth place and, during the campaign, Allan won his nineteenth and final cap, as a substitute against Portugal in Lisbon.

Leeds United squad, 1975/76. From left to right, back row: Armfield (manager), McKenzie, Jordan, McQueen, Harvey, Stewart, Madeley, Hunter, Reaney. Front row: Yorath, Gray F., Gray E., Lorimer, Cherry, Bremner, Clarke.

Allan scores his second goal of the season in a win over Wolves.

Another goal, this time the second in a 2-0 win over Coventry.

Allan scores his 100th League goal for Leeds in a 1-0 win over Aston Villa.

Billy Bremner walks over to congratulate Allan after his century of League goals.

The 1976/77 Leeds team ended the League campaign tenth as FA Cup glory beckoned once again. Allan was still an integral part of the side, but was carrying a troublesome injury.

Just after the start of the 1976/77 season I was having a bit of pain in my left knee. After a while, as it wasn't clearing up, I had some X-rays to establish where the trouble was. I got the results around Christmas and knew I needed an operation. Jimmy Armfield asked me if I'd carry on playing while we were in the FA Cup, which I was happy to do – I'm not sure it did my knee any good though.

After wins over Norwich and Birmingham City we faced Manchester City at Elland Road. In a cracking match a replay seemed inevitable, especially after Joe Corrigan had made an unbelievable save from a header of mine, but Trevor Cherry became the hero moments later when he toe-poked a late winner. In the quarter-final, Eddie scored a great header to put us within one game of my fifth FA Cup final, but it wasn't to be. We got off to a terrible start by letting in two early goals, and although we came back into the game when I converted a second half penalty we were well beaten. This was my fifth semi-final and first defeat at that stage. It was a sickening feeling.

My season was over and I had my knee operation at Leeds General Infirmary the following Sunday. On the Monday the surgeon came to see me and told me how it had gone. I'd had a cyst removed from a cartilage, and there was a lot of wear and tear due to the strain my knee had taken over the years, but it had been cleaned up and there was no reason why I could not resume playing after rehabilitation. I was quite happy with that and decided to miss a summer holiday that year, recuperate and start my pre-season early in a bid to be ready for the new campaign.

Allan battles for possession in a 2-2 draw with West Brom.

Allan displays his ice-cool finishing skills and gives Pat Jennings no chance.

Another FA Cup goal, this time against Birmingham.

Referee Bill Gow moves in to calm tempers as Leeds' FA Cup clash with Manchester City threatens to erupt.

Come on referee!

A chance goes begging in Leeds' semi-final against their rivals from Old Trafford.

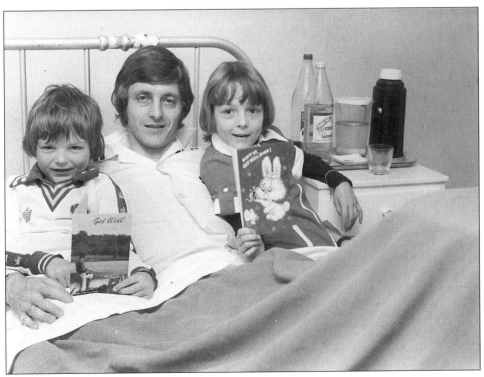

James and Sarah help Allan recuperate following a knee operation.

Leeds United squad, 1977/78. From left to right, back row: Hankin, Harris, Cherry, McQueen, Harvey, Stewart, Clarke, Jordan, Currie, Reaney. Front row: Hampton, McNiven, Graham, Lorimer, Gray E., Stevenson, Madeley, Gray F.

The referee intervenes after yet another flare-up in Allan's first game back after injury against Manchester City in the FA Cup.

Allan gets the better of 'Chopper' Harris in a 2-0 home win.

Allan scored his 150th goal for Leeds in their 5-0 thumping of Middlesborough. It was also his last full game at Elland Road.

When the lads came back for pre-season training, I was nowhere near full fitness. Whenever I ran at full pace there was a terrible pain behind my knee, I was also getting pain at the front of the knee when I tried building up my quads with weights. I was going in every day and training on my own but getting nowhere. I went to see Jimmy and the club doctor and told them I was really struggling. Doc Burridge couldn't diagnose how bad my injury was, so suggested I see a retired orthopaedic surgeon, Professor Smiley, in Scotland. I went to see him with all my medical notes and he told me if I wanted to play again I'd have to build my quads up, but it would not be easy. With that I started training again and played in a friendly against PSV Eindhoven at Elland Road. Although I scored, the sharpness to my game had gone; in that split second when the mind says go, my body just wouldn't react. I knew my days in the top flight were nearly over.

Allan spent much of his last season at Leeds on the sidelines, but he did play a few games during the 1977/78 campaign, which Leeds finished in ninth place. His first match back after injury was an FA Cup tie against Manchester City.

It proved to be a disaster. David Harvey and Gordon McQueen had to be separated after exchanging punches, and our fans invaded the pitch in a bid to stop the match. We lost 2-1. The highlights during my final few games was scoring the winner at Old Trafford in a League encounter and my 150th goal for Leeds at home to Middlesborough – the match in which I also scored my last ever goal for the club.

13

FIRST STEPS
1978-1981

For Allan, the time had come to find a new challenge. It arrived during the close season when he was approached about becoming Barnsley's player-manager.

I still had two years of my contract to go and was due a testimonial, but I knew my playing days at the top level was over. I was put under no pressure to leave, but I couldn't sit in the reserves and wait for a pay-day – it just wasn't my style. Leeds gave me permission to speak to Barnsley, and I grasped the opportunity, even though it meant taking a drop in wages. Although I'd discussed with the gaffer his approach to management and worked with Alf Ramsey for many years, my only experience was when I ran Collingham under-18 side in 1977. I knew it was a massive risk on the part of Barnsley's chairman, Ernest Dennis

After signing for £45,000, my first appointment was to reinstate Norman Rimmington as physio. Norman was groundsman, but had given his life to the club and by all accounts was thrilled when Ernest told him he'd be working for me; he was convinced Barnsley would make rapid progress. I headed straight into Barnsley town centre and asked people what they wanted from their football club, and more importantly what would entice them back to Oakwell.

The overwhelming message was clear. Some people had started going to Hillsborough, Bramall Lane and even Elland Road, but the more I talked the greater the feeling I had that local people would prefer to watch their home town club. Previous Barnsley managers had promised all sorts, but no one had delivered. I told everyone if I made a promise I would deliver.

I knew it wouldn't be easy because Barnsley was in the Fourth Division and, without being unkind, Oakwell was a dump. My first task was to give the ground a lick of paint, then I arranged for our laundry ladies to not only wash the players' kits but training gear as well. I realised that we were not a top-flight outfit, but I wanted the team to feel special. I wanted players to feel proud of playing for the club and wanting to be recognised in the town centre as a Barnsley footballer. The players also knew what I expected of them. I was a firm believer in discipline, and any player who fell out of line could expect a rocket.

I loved being player-manager, but did find it difficult in the early days trying to find the time to train and race around matches scouting for players. My short-term objective was to create an atmosphere where the players wanted to play for Barnsley;

Allan's management career starts with Collingham under-18s.

Striding ahead with Barnsley. Allan meets his playing staff on the first day of pre-season training, July 1978.

Barnsley FC, 1978/79.

my longer-term aim was to get the club promotion.

Starting with a 4-2 win over Halifax Town, Barnsley won their opening five fixtures. It was clear that the supporters began to think the club was on the march again, because the average gate approached 10,000. Next up was Torquay, when a crowd of 13,000 fans were in attendance, along with the BBC cameras.

Unfortunately we lost, the added expectations and pressure clearly getting to the players. After the match, Tony Gubba interviewed me in my office. I wasn't too disheartened because I knew we'd bounce back, my biggest concern was whether the crowd would stay with us. I needn't have worried – we won our next match against Huddersfield and never looked back.

In defence, Mick McCarthy (currently the Republic of Ireland manager) was developing into a solid centre-back and in attack my only two signings, Derek Bell and Tommy Graham, scored on a regular basis. Even I hadn't lost my touch in front of goal, scoring a hat-trick against Port Vale in a 6-2 win. As the season developed, we stayed among the pacesetters, especially after five consecutive wins during March.

At Easter I was keen to keep the momentum going, but it had to occur without me because I was still recovering from an injury received at Grimsby, one of our promotion rivals. Our three fixtures, two against bottom-four sides, brought just one point. I was livid and called a team meeting at Oakwell.

Barnsley meant nothing to me before I joined them, but I was now on the verge of guiding them to promotion. Norman told me the club had been in this position

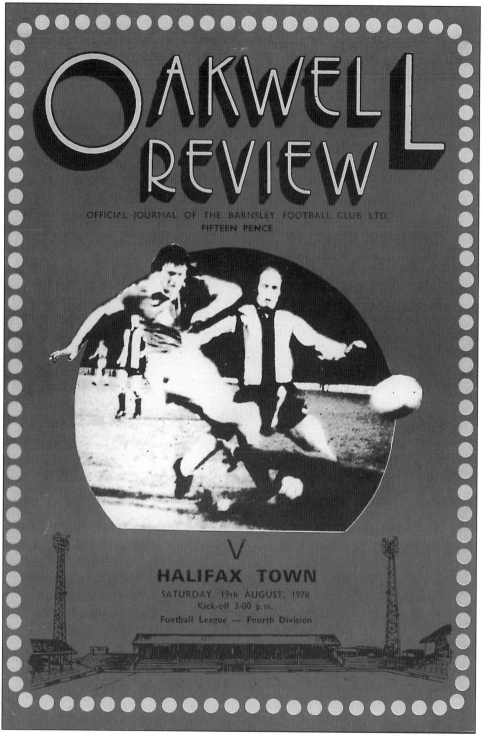

Programme from Allan's opening League game as a manager against Halifax.

Match programme, Barnsley v. Port Vale.

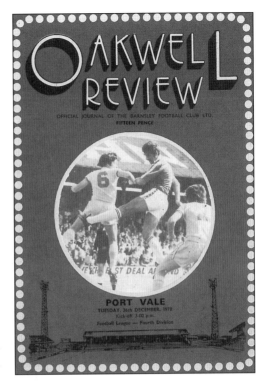

during the past two campaigns, but had fallen away at the death. The team had a great bunch of lads, but they had to know how serious I was. I told them in no uncertain terms that if we missed out on promotion a number of them would be looking for new clubs and would miss the opportunity of playing at a higher level.

At Portsmouth, a favourable result would guarantee promotion. The players responded brilliantly to win 1-0, Derek Bell striking the vital goal. It was a fabulous journey home. Our final match at home was against Grimsby. Over 21,000 fans packed Oakwell to witness our 2-1 victory. I was really pleased for the players, who had proved to themselves that they could achieve success at this level.

I took the whole squad into the main stand to thank the fans. You could not see a blade of grass. Ernest joined us; he wasn't well at the time so he held on to me for support – he was shaking with excitement. It was a wonderful night for the club. Our last match at Wimbledon was now irrelevant.

Barnsley finished the campaign in fourth place on goal difference, having finished on the same points total as Grimsby and Wimbledon.

Allan heads home for Barnsley's second goal against York City.

THE OFFICIAL PROGRAMME OF PORTSMOUTH FOOTBALL CLUB LTD.   15p

MATCH SPONSORED BY JOHN BLUNDELL LTD

Portsmouth FC versus Barnsley

Saturday, May 5, 1979
Kick Off 3pm

LEAGUE DIV. 4
78-79
SEASON

Match programme from Barnsley's crunch match at Portsmouth.

The Mayor of Barnsley gives a civic reception to the victorious Barnsley team following their promotion success.

The Barnsley Chronicle's *promotion special.*

Reading ended the season as champions.

During the summer break Ernest died. I will always remember him with enormous respect. Without his confidence in me I would not have had my opportunity in management, and I was pleased he witnessed his Barnsley side finally have some success.

Things were really going for me, and at the Footballer of the Year dinner I was asked if I'd be interested in the Sunderland job. Arthur Cox advised me to take it because Sunderland was a club with massive potential, he also offered to be my coach. I thought about it for a few days, but decided I needed more experience. I hadn't seen the flip-side of management yet, which I knew would come. I declined Sunderland's approach and looked forward to the new campaign in the Third Division with Barnsley.

At the start of the 1979/80 season, I decided that the lads who had won us promotion must be given a chance, even though I'd already made plans in my own mind on where I needed to strengthen the team if they failed to adapt. We struggled, losing four of our opening matches.

At Barnsley, we had a board meeting every two weeks. For the past year I'd been told how well things were going, and most importantly how financially we were on the up due to the increased gates. However, the directors soon made it clear they were not happy with results. My response was blunt. I'd proved I could do the job; I had the backing of the supporters, now I needed to know if I had the backing of the Board. I gave them an ultimatum – either they lie down and die or let me rebuild.

Barnsley FC 1979/80.

BARNSLEY F.C.

OFFICIAL MATCH DAY MAGAZINE 20p

OAKWELL REVIEW

BLACKPOOL

League Division 3   Friday, 21st December, 1979, 7-30 p.m.

Match programme: Barnsley v. Blackpool. Allan scored his last goal as a player.

Match programme: Reading v. Barnsley. Allan's last game as a player.

The Barnsley management team show Barnsley's players life from a different perspective – down Wooley Colliery.

To their credit the Board backed me and I strengthened the squad with the likes of Ronnie Glavin, Bobby Downs, Trevor Aylott and Mike Lester. The players gelled with promising youngsters like Mick McCarthy and Ian Banks and results soon improved.

During the season I scored my last League goal, at Oakwell in our 2-1 win over Blackpool, and retired a week later following a 7-0 thrashing at Reading to concentrate on management full time. It's ironic that my last match as a player was against Reading, because my League debut for Walsall was also against them. As they say, it's a funny old game!

After the Reading defeat I was furious and wanted the players to know what real life and working hard for a living was all about. I arranged for the whole squad to spend a day at Woolley colliery, which had closed down and was nearby. We met at six in the morning. They spoke with miners who had worked at the colliery for years, and there was plenty of murmuring when the players descended into the filthy pit. They had to know how lucky they were to be professional football players.

It got the reaction I wanted. We moved away from trouble and finished the season strongly, winning four of our last six games. We ended the campaign in eleventh place and I couldn't wait for the new one to begin. I genuinely believed Barnsley were in a position for a tilt at promotion.

14

BACK HOME
1981/82

Barnsley built on the progress made the previous season, but speculation was mounting that Allan would be replacing Jimmy Adamson as manager at Leeds United.

I was really pleased at how Barnsley had begun the campaign, after six games they were lying second in the table and looked comfortable. Leeds United, meanwhile, had approached me to become manager; I told them to go through the proper channels. I was given permission to talk with Leeds. Whilst I was excited at the prospect, I was disappointed that Barnsley didn't really attempt to keep me.

Before I met Manny Cussins, my assistant, Martin Wilkinson, produced a dossier for me on the current Leeds side, who were lying second bottom of the First Division. A big rebuilding job was required to make Leeds a force again – I'd need six players. I was offered £2 million to spend; it wasn't a fortune – Brian Clough had just spent £1 million on Birmingham City's Trevor Francis – but it would enable me to buy three good players to begin with. I agreed to become Leeds United's new manager.

I went back to Barnsley to tie up a few loose ends and inform my players, which I did at the end of our next match at Brentford. There was sadness on both parts, but I could not turn down this opportunity and the players understood that. I told them to finish the job they'd started that season and win promotion, which they did.

Returning to Leeds was never going to be easy. The team had won only one game and was playing with little confidence. In addition, gates had steadily fallen for a few seasons and were now down to under 20,000. The supporters were well and truly disillusioned. Allan would also have to manage former team-mates like Trevor Cherry, Eddie Gray, Paul Hart, Arthur Graham and Carl Harris.

On my first day as manager I had a meeting with all the players. I told them there would be no favouritism, there was time to pull clear of relegation and I would take a view on everyone in the squad. My first priority was to improve their fitness, which was worse than that of the players I'd left at Barnsley.

We began well by drawing against Manchester United, but then got thrashed at Sunderland. The following week during training, our left-back, Byron Stevenson, picked up an injury. I asked Eddie Gray to deputise in a twenty-minute practice match. He was a revelation. I played him against Ipswich and he kept his place for

One of Allan's last games in charge at Oakwell. Here he watches his charges against Huddersfield.

At home with the family in 1980.

The new manager of Leeds United: Allan Clarke, with his assistant manager Martin Wilkinson and coach Barry Murphy.

Leeds United's new manager leads out his team for his first game in charge, against Manchester United.

The Kop welcome their hero home!

the rest of the season. Eddie was brilliant in tandem with Arthur Graham and was by far the best left-back in the League. This decision extended his playing career by three seasons and it enabled me to revise my thoughts on who to purchase.

We slowly moved up the table with a system that wasn't the prettiest to watch, but suited the players. Towards the end of the season, Ipswich came to Elland Road as League leaders. They strolled into the ground with an attitude that they would win comfortably, and played as if they'd already taken the title. We won 3-0. I knew we were on the right lines and looked to strengthen the team. My priorities were a full-back, a striker and a winger.

At the end of the campaign I enquired about Frank Gray and I arranged to meet Brian Clough and Peter Taylor at Nottingham Forest. Forest wanted £450,000, but were stretched financially so I offered £300,000. They weren't happy. I told them my valuation and began to leave the room, then Brian shook my hand. Frank came to my home next morning where we agreed terms. I went to see the Board that afternoon – they were thrilled.

Peter Barnes became available and I spent £930,000 on him. After informing the Board of this they told me no more money was available. I was stunned – I'd only spent £1.2 million of my budget. Looking back, I wish the Board had been more open

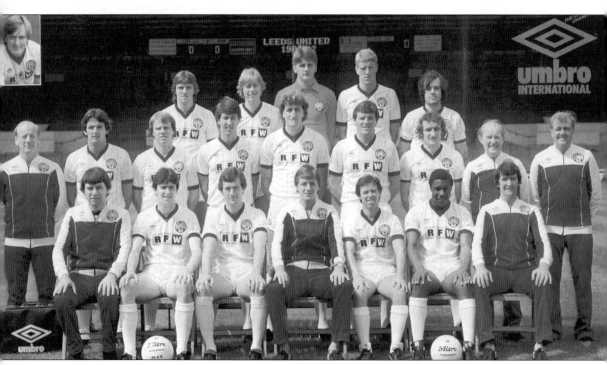

Leeds United, 1981/82. From left to right, back row: Harris, Greenhoff, Lukic, Firm, Sabella. Middle row: Ladley (physio), Gray F., Graham, Parlane, Hart, Gray E., Hird, English (kit manager), Gumby (coach). Front row: Wilkinson (assistant manager), Stevenson, Cherry, Clarke (manager), Flynn, Connor, Murphy (coach) Inset: Barnes.

Worried looks all round as Clarke's team scrapes a 3-3 draw with West Ham.

with me. If I'd known the cash flow situation I would not have bought Peter Barnes because I needed a striker more. The player I wanted was Gary Thompson of Coventry, but he wasn't available at the time.

I had a serious problem now because throughout the previous campaign we'd struggled to score goals and I still only had Carl Harris, Derek Parlane and Aiden Butterworth at my disposal, which wasn't good enough.

We began the 1981/82 season atrociously, winning just one of our opening ten games. I was allowed to buy Kenny Burns to help shore up our defence as Jeff Chandler and Alex Sabella moved on. We were deep in a relegation battle, so I traded Byron Stevenson for Frank Worthington, which brought some dividends, but I still had an unbalanced team.

My major headache was Peter Barnes. On his day he could be brilliant, however the game was changing and part of his role was to help out in defence, but he rarely did. During the season I dropped him. The Board then interfered and demanded I play him, but I refused till he justified his place. I brought him back for the run-in, but I was still unhappy. I told the Board certain players had to go. Manny told me he'd heard there was unrest in the dressing room, but would not co-operate. At that moment my time at Leeds was over: the Board had lost faith in me. Although we occasionally rallied, it was touch and go whether we'd survive.

Going into the final game our destiny was still in our hands. Our final match was

Allan departs from Elland Road for the last time as manager.

at West Brom – a win and we were safe. Everyone should have been prepared to sweat buckets that afternoon, but certain players were a disgrace and did not deserve to wear a Leeds United shirt. We lost 2-0.

After the game, people like Terry Connor were inconsolable; for others it was just another game. Our only hope of avoiding relegation was if West Brom beat Stoke in their last game. I went to the match. I should have stayed at home – only Derek Statham tried, the rest might as well have sat in the stand with me. I was devastated.

A few days later I was due to go on holiday. I was summoned to a board meeting and told it would be taken badly if I didn't attend. I was mentally shattered and needed a rest. I missed the meeting. After returning from Portugal I went to the next board meeting. We discussed where things had gone wrong. I told them it all stemmed from the time I got no backing over troublesome players. I was handed a list of conditions I would have to work under during the next campaign. I knew my days were over at Leeds, which saddened me because I loved the club. The next day I met Manny Cussins and we sorted matters out amicably.

Looking back, I still believe that if the Board had taken a longer-term view things may have been different. I was always a firm believer in a youth policy and in the short period I was at the club a number of players showed tremendous promise. Apprentices who went on to have fine careers included David Seaman, Dennis Irwin, Scott Sellars, Terry Phelan, Neil Aspin, John Sheridan and Tommy Wright.

My time as manager of Leeds United was very disappointing, but I'm pleased I had the chance and it certainly hasn't affected my feelings for the club. I still go to every home game and get a tremendous welcome every time. I'm only sorry I wasn't given the opportunity to try getting them back into the First Division.

15

BACK TO THE BASEMENT
1983/84

Despite his disappointing time at Elland Road, Allan was keen to find another managerial job.

Eight months after leaving Leeds I received a call from David Wraith, chairman of Scunthorpe United. He wanted me to become their manager. They were near the fringes of promotion but, after being knocked out of the FA Cup, had parted company with their manager, John Duncan. I told him I'd watch their next game from the terraces. The following day I accepted the job.

At my first home game against Bristol City, I wasn't given a particularly warm welcome because supporters saw John Duncan's departure as a huge shock. This disappointed both David and myself, because I had nothing to do with his dismissal. We drew and I made my feelings known that the squad was not strong enough to mount a sustained promotion push.

The players surprised me by embarking on a great run. Of our first ten games we lost just once. I signed Mike Lester and Tommy Graham, who both settled into the team to support Steve Cammack in attack. We stayed in contention.

Scunthorpe were outsiders for promotion, because they were dependent on other teams slipping up, but kept up the pressure. A last-minute winner against Blackpool by Steve Cammack was followed by victories over Peterborough, Swindon and Port Vale. A win at Chester in the final game of the season would clinch the final promotion place if Bury lost their last match.

We had horrendous injury problems. Scunthorpe only had a small squad and two of our regulars failed last-minute tests, so I was forced to play two apprentices, Ian Webster and Simon Shaw. The players were incredible and against all the odds we won 2-1, Tommy Graham scoring both. We waited for the Bury result. They'd lost 3-1 – we were up! I could hardly believe it.

The players had shown tremendous character and I was delighted they had proved me wrong. When you looked at the size and balance of the squad – there was no midfield player on duty at Chester – it was a miracle we were able to go up. Gaining promotion was fantastic, but my experiences at Barnsley told me the next season would be extremely difficult. The Third Division was worlds apart from the Fourth

A new beginning! David Wraith discusses the future of Scunthorpe United with the new manager.

Scunthorpe United, 1982/83.

We're up! Scunthorpe after their unbelievable promotion success.

Scunthorpe United, 1983/84.

and I was sure the present squad would not survive. I told the chairman to enjoy the weekend; we'd talk Monday morning! The following Monday he was still on a high until I asked him how much money we had to spend. There was very little. I told him I would do all I could to keep them up.

David was a great chairman and we discussed ways of funding the development of the club. He asked me if I would consider investing in Scunthorpe by becoming a director. By now I had moved into the area so the offer seemed a good opportunity. I was still responsible for team matters, and wasn't surprised that we struggled from the beginning of the campaign.

Scunthorpe won just four of their opening twenty matches then stayed unbeaten during January and February, drawing six consecutive games! During this run they made unlikely progress in the FA Cup, having reached the third round stage.

After defeating Preston I was delighted with our draw in the fourth round: away to Leeds. Even though they were no more than an average Second Division side at this time, my players were really looking forward to playing at Elland Road because they had never played anywhere like it.

The Leeds supporters gave me a great ovation, which really pleased me. We played exceptionally well and deserved our late equaliser from Steve Cammack. I was delighted with the result, but we were still very much the underdogs. The replay followed a similar pattern and again we equalised, both goals coming in extra time. At the end I went to the referee's room to establish the venue for a second replay. Eddie and I tossed a coin for it. Eddie lost. The Old Show Ground was filled to capacity again in anticipation of a cup upset, and we didn't disappoint, winning 4-2 for not only one of the shocks of the round but more importantly one of the most memorable nights in the club's history. In the fifth round we faced a trip to First Division West Brom and were very unlucky to lose 1-0.

Scunthorpe's cup form began to show in the League, and towards the end of the season survival seemed a possibility until they lost three of their Easter fixtures. Though Burnley were beaten 4-0 in the final home game of the season, just one point from their remaining two matches meant relegation. The Burnley win was one of only nine all season and none had been achieved away from home. During the close season, Allan tried to prepare for the new campaign, but hit a number of obstacles. All attempts to sign new players were thwarted and there was a power struggle in the boardroom.

David informed me he was selling his business. Tom Belton took over as chairman and David and myself left. There was no way I was going to stay where I wasn't wanted, so I left them to it.

Allan points the way during his side's brilliant 1-1 draw in the FA Cup at Elland Road.

*Match programme from
Scunthope's sensational 4-2 win
over Leeds.*

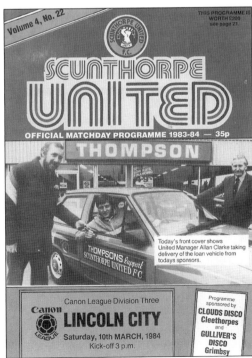

*Match programme during
Scunthorpe's unsuccessful bid to
avoid relegation.*

16

CUP BATTLES GALORE
1985-1989

After leaving Scunthorpe, Allan worked briefly at David Wraith's company. After a season out of the game, Geoff Buckle of Barnsley offered him the chance of returning as manager for a second spell.

Barnsley was still in the Second Division. I chatted with supporters and it soon became obvious that I would be inheriting a relegation side with no money to spend. I accepted the challenge.

After an opening day defeat at Charlton, where teenager David Hirst made his debut, Barnsley began the campaign brightly. By the return fixture in December, where Hirst grabbed both goals in Barnsley's 2-1 win, the side were fourth in the table. Unfortunately the second half of the campaign would be far less fruitful, with just four victories being achieved. Barnsley finished the season in twelfth place.

Two of our best performances during our League campaign were against Leeds. We thumped them 3-0 at Oakwell and later that season, when Billy had replaced Eddie as manager, we completed the double with a 2-0 win. It may sound daft, but although I was delighted with the win I didn't get the same satisfaction beating Leeds as another club because I still had a great deal of affection for the Leeds supporters.

Running a club at this level was always a balancing act of consolidation and discovering a potential star that could be sold to finance the next stage of development. Managers used to ring me all the time and I knew that all my best players could be snapped up because we could not refuse a reasonable offer. We were a club that nurtured players and I had to accept that.

At Barnsley the pick of the younger players was our centre forward David Hirst, who I reluctantly sold to Sheffield Wednesday for £250,000 during the close season. In one swoop our overdraft was gone. The players knew the situation and as long as they gave me everything on the football pitch I would not deny them the chance to make a name for themselves, which David did in the top league for many seasons.

In 1986/87 Barnsley lost their opening six games but came back well in the second half of the season to finish eleventh. In the cups they were drawn against some of the game's biggest clubs. Such glamour ties would become the norm over the next three

Barnsley FC, 1985/86.

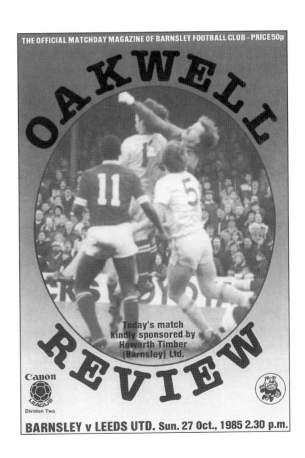

Match programme from Barnsley's 3-0 win over Leeds.

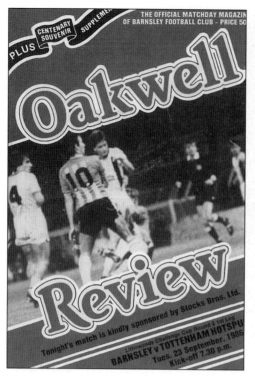

Programme from Barnsley's 3-2 defeat by high-flying Tottenham.

Programme from Barnsley's tremendous 5-2 win at West Ham.

Barnsley FC, 1987/88.

Programme from Barnsley's encounter with Chelsea when the Londoners were thumped 4-0 in the FA Cup.

Allan during the pre-season of 1989/90.

The Clarke family today.

seasons for the Barnsley faithful…

We drew Tottenham in the League Cup. In the first leg we came back strongly after letting in an early goal to lead 2-1, but two late goals gave them the advantage. At White Hart Lane, we lost a thrilling match 5-3 and came out with a lot of credit, especially when you consider Tottenham reached the FA Cup final that season. In the FA Cup the draw favoured us and after defeating Caernarfon and Aldershot drew a plum tie at Arsenal in the fifth round. Although we battled hard we lost 2-0.

Barnsley began the 1987/88 season in fine form, winning four of the opening six games. They then drew West Ham in the League Cup.

Our experiences in the cup competitions the previous season certainly helped. In the first leg at Oakwell we were not overawed at all and were a little unlucky to draw 0-0. In the return, though, we put in an unbelievable display, winning 5-2. In the third round we faced our local rivals, Sheffield Wednesday, at Hillsborough. Unfortunately we lost a really tight match 2-1.

In the League, however, Barnsley became really inconsistent. After a couple of wins they'd struggle, the cycle repeating itself throughout the winter months. The season became a real slog and two wins in their final ten games of the season saw them finish fourteenth.

Barnsley's poor form continued when the 1988/89 campaign began, but five victories in October, beginning with a 5-3 thumping over Birmingham, pushed them into the play-off places. Four goals from David Currie against Bournemouth in a 5-2 win were part of another surge of wins before the New Year. The players and Allan turned their attentions to the FA Cup.

We drew Chelsea at home in the third round. Having lost narrowly to Wimbledon in the League Cup earlier in the season, I really felt we could cause an upset. Before the match we made sure that our visitors' dressing room was less luxurious than normal! Whether the psychology worked I'm not sure, but we thumped them 4-0 for a wonderful win. Sadly, one incident marred the match when one of our key players, Gwyn Thomas, was hacked down. He missed the rest of the season and played only a handful of games for Barnsley again. It brought no punishment and soured a great win for me.

In the next round we drew at Stoke City 3-3 after leading by two goals, but redeemed ourselves in the replay, winning 2-1. We then drew Everton in the fifth round, which was a bit special for me because my younger brother Wayne was due to play for them – unfortunately he missed out through injury. They had a super team and we ran them close, losing to a solitary goal. I was really proud of the players, because Everton not only reached the final that year but also won the First Division Championship.

After losing to Everton it took a while for the players to find their League form again, which proved very costly. Following a seven-game run without a win, Sunderland were defeated 3-0, sparking a tremendous run of form which generated seven wins in the last nine matches and took Barnsley to fringes of the play-offs. They missed out by just two points, ending the season in seventh place.

This would be the closest Allan would get to promotion in his second spell at Oakwell. After winning three of the opening seven games at the start of the 1989/90 season, just one win in the next ten saw Allan and Barnsley part company.

The day I left so did Geoff Buckle. It was a very sad day for Barnsley; however, they were still in the Second Division and had a healthy bank balance. Throughout my second spell I was always honest with supporters. They knew if we won promotion we'd probably be relegated immediately; they also knew I stabilised the club financially. Whenever I'm in Barnsley, fans never fail to tell me that I started the success story back in the 1970s – which is very rewarding. Looking back I had some wonderful times at the club. I was one of their more successful managers and I'm proud of that.

After a very brief spell at Lincoln, I retired from the game and have no regrets from my twelve years in football management. I did it my own way, which was maybe my downfall in some instances, but I have never been a 'yes' man. For the last nine years I have worked for MTS Nationwide, who are a plant-hire company and on weekends can be found at Elland Road in the corporate hospitality section. I watch all Leeds United's home games and act as a pundit on other occasions, which I enjoy immensely. I still look out for three results each week: Leeds United, Walsall and Barnsley.

Every spare moment that Margaret and I have is spent with our children and grandchildren. Sarah and David live close by with their two children, Luke and Kate, while James and Clare live near Wakefield. My private life has always been the stabilising influence on my professional life and has constantly reminded me that football is not a matter of life and death! Football has, however, been good to me – I've been very fortunate.

LEEDS UNITED DREAM SQUAD

For me there can only be one dream team that I would play in, but I'm picking twelve players because I can't decide on a substitute.

David Harvey *was a brave goalkeeper. Agile and a terrific shot-stopper, he handled the ball well, kept good angles and always commanded his penalty box. After he replaced Gary Sprake in goal, I always felt our defence looked more assured. David was Scotland's first choice 'keeper in the mid-70s and was chosen by the world press as the outstanding goalkeeper of the 1974 World Cup.*

Paul Reaney *was an incredibly quick right-back, especially when making recovery tackles, and he supported the attack continually with his overlapping runs. His anticipation was also first rate, which enabled him to be aware of danger at crucial moments. I lost count of the number of goals he saved with his goal-line clearances. Only injury denied him a place in England's 1970 World Cup squad, but quite rightly he won full England honours.*

Terry Cooper *was a world-class attacking left-back, and formed a wonderful understanding down the left with Eddie Gray. I was with him during the World Cup in Mexico and he was quite rightly acknowledged as the best in his position at the tournament. Terry started off as a winger, and it certainly helped him, because when he was in and around the penalty area he beat players as if they weren't there. Sadly, his Leeds career was effectively ended after a terrible leg injury just before the 1972 Cup Final.*

Billy Bremner *was undoubtedly the best player I ever played with. Billy loved being skipper of Leeds and Scotland and had it all; fitness, speed, guts and style. He was a ball-winner one moment, a goal scorer the next. Billy was at times temperamental, but that was his nature – above all he was a winner. Although he played in midfield, the ground he covered was phenomenal, his determination and enthusiasm were exceptional and many of his goals were crucial, four of them winning cup semi-finals. Acknowledged worldwide, Billy played many games when unfit but was so*

David Harvey

Paul Reaney

Terry Cooper

Billy Bremner

inspirational he couldn't be left out. Billy Bremner is by far the most famous player to pull on the white shirt of Leeds United.

His inspiration on the field was matched by our friendship off it. From the day I arrived at Elland Road, we got on incredibly well as team-mates. He pointed out in no uncertain terms that to survive at Leeds dedication was required, no matter how expensive a player was – and that was fine by me. Billy was my roommate, when he left Leeds we spoke every day, and throughout difficult periods of my life he was always the first person I'd ring. He was like a brother to me. When he died I was in shock for a long time, and no day goes by without me thinking about him. Billy was my best friend. As a footballer few bettered him, as a person he is irreplaceable.

Jack Charlton *was a terrific centre-half and I always felt happier when he was in the side: he was so solid. A master in the air, he could handle any forward and regularly man-marked opponents out of a game. Jack was a tower of strength in defence and created havoc when going forward at set-pieces. He became renowned for standing on the opposition's goal-line to unsettle the defence, scoring many goals in the process.*

Norman Hunter *was a superb defender whose bone-crunching tackles and fierce determination brought him the nickname Norman 'Bites yer legs'. However, Norman had much more to his game than just being a ferocious tackler. When in possession, Norman was a great passer of the ball and could read his opponents' reactions perfectly. Without a doubt he would have played for England many more times but for being unlucky enough to be in competition with Bobby Moore.*

Peter Lorimer *was best known for his awesome shooting power – he could really leather a ball. Fans nicknamed him 'Hot-shot' Lorimer and from forty yards out Peter was lethal. However, there was a lot more to his game. He was quick, strong, had great balance and ball control, and was an incredibly accurate crosser of the ball. Peter was a winger, not a central striker, so the number of goals he scored was phenomenal. Still the record goal scorer for Leeds, he also represented Scotland on many occasions.*

As for me, I've decided to use Billy's thoughts, which Vicky kindly me gave permission to use. 'Allan was a great passer of the ball and had great ball control. I also found it amazing how incredibly calm he was in front of goal. He rarely missed a one-on-one opportunity; he was such a clinical finisher. Allan was invaluable to the side, and from the time he joined Leeds United he gave us more attacking options than we ever had before. He was an inspirational signing for us and scored many crucial goals, especially the one in the '72 Cup Final.'

Mick Jones *was the best striking-partner I played with for either club or country. From our first game together we complemented each other's style of play. Jonah was the target man and chased any lost cause. He had terrific close control and used his*

Jack Charlton

Norman Hunter

Peter Lorimer

Allan Clarke

strength to hold the ball up while I looked for space to support him. If I was being man-marked I'd go deeper to pick balls up. Any crosses that came into the box one of us would attack the near post; the other would peel off to the back-stick. He was a brilliant header of the ball and scored his fair share of goals. Jonah quite rightly played for England, I'm only sorry Alf never picked us to play together at the highest level. We were compared with Toshack and Keegan of Liverpool, Radford and Kennedy of Arsenal, Chivers and Gilzean of Tottenham, and Osgood and Baldwin of Chelsea. None of them touched us.

John Giles *was one of the most creative players of his era. He was a clinical passer of the ball and knew instinctively where to hurt our opponents. He could also look after himself! A master at reading a game and spreading play, he developed a telepathic understanding with Billy and together they became one of the most feared midfield combinations in Europe. The biggest compliment I can give John is that he was the nearest in pure footballing ability to Johnny Haynes.*

Eddie Gray *is without doubt the most naturally gifted footballer I played with and scored one of the best goals I ever saw against Burnley in 1970. Eddie could do anything with a football: his dribbling skills were unbelievable and he could unlock any defence. Unfortunately, Eddie was unlucky with injuries, which limited his appearances for Leeds and Scotland. People talk about George Best, yet Eddie had as much ability. During those times we were under pressure and needed someone to hold the ball, we used Eddie because we knew he'd be so difficult to dispossess. He was some player.*

Paul Madeley *may be the twelfth player mentioned, but he was no substitute. Paul was always in the team at either left-back, right-back, centre-back or midfield – due to an injury, suspension or tactical reasoning. Undoubtedly the most versatile footballer of his era, Paul could play anywhere. He didn't have electric pace but his long stride ate the ground up. Paul was strong, fit and a fabulous player to have in your side. Invaluable, he played for England many times, despite having no recognised position at club level, which says it all.*

As for the gaffer, ***Don Revie****, he was quite simply the biggest influence on my career and enabled me to play in a side where I was able to achieve my ambitions. Playing in this team was so easy and such a pleasure because there was so much ability in the side. Whether we were at home or away we got at teams, it was impossible to sit back. We played some scintillating stuff. During my time at Leeds United we won the title once, came runners-up three times and third once. In addition we got to three FA Cup and three European finals. That's some record and one I'm very proud to be associated with.*

Mick Jones

Johnny Giles

Eddy Grey

Paul Madeley

ALLAN CLARKE'S CAREER STATISTICS

Football League Playing Career

Club	Season	League Division	League Apps	League Goals	League Position	FA Cup Apps	FA Cup Goals	FA Cup Round	L Cup Apps	L Cup Goals	L Cup Round	Europe Apps	Europe Goals	Europe Round	Other Apps	Other Goals	Total Apps	Total Goals	Top Scorer
Walsall	1963/64	Three	6	0	19	-	-	-	-	-	-	-	-	-	-	-	6	0	
Walsall	1964/65	Three	43	23	19	-	-	-	-	-	-	-	-	-	-	-	43	23	*
Walsall	1965/66	Three	24	19	9	2	1	4	3	1	2	-	-	-	-	-	29	21	*
Summary			73	42		2	1	4	3	1	2	-	-	-	-	-	78	44	
Fulham	1965/66	One	7(1)	0	20	-	-	-	-	-	-	-	-	-	-	-	7(1)	0	
Fulham	1966/67	One	42	24	18	3	3	4	2	2	4	-	-	-	-	-	47	29	*
Fulham	1967/68	One	36	20	22	3	2	4	6	5	5	-	-	-	-	-	45	27	*
Summary			85(1)	44		6	5		8	7		-	-	-	-	-	99(1)	56	
Leicester City	1968/69	One	36	12	21	8	1	F	2	3	4	-	-	-	-	-	46	16	*
Summary			36	12		8	1	F	2	3	4	-	-	-	-	-	46	16	
Leeds United	1969/70	One	28	17	2	9	7	F	-	-	-	5	2	S/F	1	0	43	26	*
Leeds United	1970/71	One	41	19	2	4	1	5	1	-	2	10	3	W	-	-	56	23	*
Leeds United	1971/72	One	35	11	2	6	4	W	2	-	3	-	-	-	-	-	43	15	
Leeds United	1972/73	One	36	18	3	8	6	F	4	-	4	5	2	F	-	-	53	26	*
Leeds United	1973/74	One	34	13	1	2(1)	-	5	-	-	-	5	3	3	-	-	41(1)	16	
Leeds United	1974/75	One	33(1)	14	9	7	3	Q/F	3	1	4	8	4	F	1	0	52(1)	22	
Leeds United	1975/76	One	35(1)	11	5	2	1	4	1	1	3	-	-	-	-	-	38(1)	13	
Leeds United	1976/77	One	20	4	10	5	3	S/F	1	-	2	-	-	-	-	-	26	7	
Leeds United	1977/78	One	8(1)	3	9	0(1)	-	3	1	-	S/F	-	-	-	-	-	9(2)	3	
Summary			270(3)	110		43(2)	25		13	2		33	14		2	0	361(5)	151	
Barnsley	1978/79	Four	34	12	4	3	2	2	2	0	1	-	-	-	-	-	39	14	
Barnsley	1979/80	Three	13	3	11	2	1	2	1	0	2	-	-	-	-	-	16	4	
Summary			47	15		5	3		3	0		-	-	-	-	-	55	18	

Debut games	Opposition	Date	Competition
Walsall	Reading	3-Oct-63	Division Three
Fulham	Leeds United	8-Apr-66	Division One
Leicester	QPR	10-Aug-68	Division One
Leeds United	Manchester City	2-Aug-69	Charity Shield
Barnsley	Chesterfield	12-Aug-78	League Cup

International Playing Career

Level	Date	Competition	Opposition	Venue	Score	Goals	Attendance
England Under-23	12-Oct-66	Friendly	Wales Under-23	Molineux, Wolves	8-0	4	
England Under-23	10-May-67	Friendly	Austria Under-23	Boothferry Park, Hull	3-0		
England Under-23	31-May-67	Friendly	Greece Under-23	Athens	0-0		10,000
England Under-23	3-Jun-67	Friendly	Bulgaria Under-23	Sofia	1-1		
England Under-23	7-Jun-67	Friendly	Turkey Under-23	Ankara	3-0	1	25,000
England Under-23	16-Apr-69	Friendly	Portugal Under-23	Highfield Rd., Coventry	4-0	2	13,631
England XI	4-Jun-69	Friendly	Mexico XI	Guadalajara	4-0	2	45,000
England 'B'	20-May-70	Friendly	Colombia	Bogata	1-0		28,000
England 'B'	24-May-70	Friendly	Universitaria	Quito	4-1		22,250
England	11-Jun-70	World Cup Finals	Czechoslovakia	Guadalajara	1-0	1 pen	49,000
England	12-Nov-70	Friendly	East Germany	Wembley	3-1	1	93,000
England	12-May-71	European Championship	Malta	Wembley	5-0	1 pen	36,000
England	15-May-71	Home International	Northern Ireland	Belfast	1-0	1	33,500
England	19-May-71	Home International	Wales (sub)	Wembley	0-0		70,000
England	22-May-71	Home International	Scotland (sub)	Wembley	3-1		91,469
England	14-Feb-73	Friendly	Scotland	Hampden Park	5-0	2	48,470
England	15-May-73	Home International	Wales	Wembley	3-0		39,000
England	19-May-73	Home International	Scotland	Wembley	1-0		95,950
England	27-May-73	Friendly	Czechoslovakia	Prague	1-1	1	25,000
England	6-Jun-73	World Cup Qual Rd	Poland	Chorzow	0-2		118,000
England	10-Jun-73	Friendly	USSR	Moscow	2-1		85,000
England	14-Jun-73	Friendly	Italy	Turin	0-2		52,000
England	26-Sep-73	Friendly	Austria	Wembley	7-0	2	48,000
England	17-Oct-73	World Cup Qual Rd	Poland	Wembley	1-1	1 pen	100,000
England	14-Nov-73	Friendly	Italy	Wembley	0-2		95,000
England	20-Nov-74	European Champ (Qual)	Portugal	Wembley	0-0		70,750
England	30-Oct-75	European Champ (Qual)	Czechoslovakia	Bratislavia	1-2		45,000
England	19-Nov-75	European Champ (Qual)	Portugal (sub)	Lisbon	1-1		30,000

Football League Managerial Career

Club	Competition	Season	P	W	D	L	F	A	Pts	Position	Round
Barnsley	Division Four	1978/79	46	24	13	9	73	42	61	4	-
Barnsley	FA Cup	1978/79	3	1	1	1	7	4	-	-	2
Barnsley	League Cup	1978/79	2	0	1	1	1	2	-	-	1
Barnsley	Division Three	1979/80	46	16	14	16	53	56	46	11	-
Barnsley	FA Cup	1979/80	2	1	0	1	5	3	-	-	2
Barnsley	League Cup	1979/80	4	1*	0	3	4	8	-	-	2
Barnsley^	Division Three	1980/81	7	3	2	2	8	8	11	-	-
Barnsley	League Cup	1980/81	4	3	1	0	7	3	-	-	4
			114	49	32	33	158	126	118		
Leeds United	Division One	1980/81	36	16	9	11	34	35	41	9	-
Leeds United	FA Cup	1980/81	2	0	1	1	1	2	-	-	3
Leeds United	Division One	1981/82	42	10	12	20	39	61	42	20	-
Leeds United	FA Cup	1981/82	2	1	0	1	3	2	-	-	4
Leeds United	League Cup	1981/82	2	0	0	2	0	4	-	-	2
			84	27	22	35	77	104	83		
Scunthorpe	Division Four	1982/83	20	10	6	4	34	22	36	4	-
Scunthorpe	Division Three	1983/84	46	9	19	18	54	73	46	21	-
Scunthorpe	FA Cup	1983/84	6	3	2	1	9	5	-	-	4
Scunthorpe	League Cup	1983/84	2	0	1	1	1	4	-	-	1
Scunthorpe	Associate Members Cup	1983/84	3	1	1**	1	8	8	-	-	3
			77	23	29	25	106	112	82		
Barnsley	Division Two	1985/86	42	14	14	14	47	50	56	12	-
Barnsley	FA Cup	1985/86	1	0	0	1	0	2	-	-	3
Barnsley	League Cup	1985/86	2	0	2***	0	1	1	-	-	2
Barnsley	Division Two	1986/87	42	14	13	15	49	52	55	11	-
Barnsley	FA Cup	1986/87	5	2	2	1	5	3	-	-	5
Barnsley	League Cup	1986/87	2	0	0	2	5	8	-	-	2
Barnsley	Full Members Cup	1986/87	1	0	1**	0	1	1	-	-	1
Barnsley	Division Two	1987/88	44	15	12	17	61	62	57	14	-
Barnsley	FA Cup	1987/88	2	1	0	1	3	3	-	-	4
Barnsley	League Cup	1987/88	3	1	1	1	6	4	-	-	3
Barnsley	Full Members Cup	1987/88	1	0	0	1	1	2	-	-	1
Barnsley	Division Two	1988/89	46	20	14	12	66	58	74	7	-
Barnsley	FA Cup	1988/89	4	2	1	1	9	5	-	-	5
Barnsley	League Cup	1988/89	2	1	0	1	1	2	-	-	2
Barnsley	Full Members Cup	1988/89	1	0	1**	0	1	1	-	-	1
Barnsley^	Division Two	1989/90	16	4	4	8	19	31	16	-	-
Barnsley	League Cup	1989/90	2	0	2**	0	2	2	-	-	2
			216	74	67	75	277	287	258		

*match won on toss of coin
**match lost on penalties
***match lost on away goals rule
^No final league position mentioned due to Allan leaving during the season
No records are available for Allan's brief spell at Lincoln City